PERFORMANCE MANAGEMENT
– It's all you need!

Bob Kent

2000

To Lynda Pavlik for showing me the way
and being a model of personal discipline.

To my granddaghter Alicia for being the inspiration
for me to keep going when times have been tough.

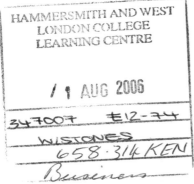
First published in 2004 by Management Books 2000 Ltd
Forge House, Limes Road
Kemble, Cirencester
Gloucestershire, GL7 6AD, UK
Tel: 0044 (0) 1285 771441/2
Fax: 0044 (0) 1285 771055
E-mail: m.b.2000@virgin.net
Web: www.mb2000.com

Printed and bound in Great Britain by Digital Books Logistics

British Library Cataloguing in Publication Data is available
ISBN 1-85252-449-9

Preface

This book neither tries nor pretends to be an in-depth, expert model for human psychology. It may break into some illustrative examples based on experiences – but that's it. Other books are available should you wish to go further in a search for detail, specific people types and traits, or psyches and so on. However, psychologist is one of the roles the successful people manager must play.

The book *does* look at people – our colleagues, peers and managers – to identify recognisable mannerisms, attitudes, and relationships, and reactions to various business environments.

It *does* propose the understanding of people in a business, as fundamental to getting the best results out of them.

The book is not a management manual. Quite the reverse. It offers a guideline approach to getting results by recognising people, what they do, what they can do, how they best operate, and how to maintain control of business direction whilst maximising their contribution in an environment of free expression.

Based on experience and observation, *Performance Management – It's all you need!* offers a platform for People Managers upon which individuals can succeed with minimum close supervision.

The basis, throughout, remains the application of common sense, simplicity and clarity of understanding – a reverse advocation, it would seem, of the many management theories, concepts and buzz words that continue to be poured onto the conveyor belt from Academialand and onto our desks.

Yes, some acronyms are used, but hopefully under the umbrella of common sense, simplicity and clarity of understanding.

5

About the author

Bob Kent is currently responsible for Customer Service at a Security Technology Company in Birmingham.

This follows a 4-year period in Interim Management. His previous permanent position was Commercial Director with a paperback book manufacturer.

He has worked in a variety of industries and occupied positions in sales, production control, work study, quality, materials stock control, customer service, purchasing logistics and IT.

Bob gained his greatest understanding of, and indeed interest in, people when working amongst predominantly graduates at Digital Equipment Company. This was indeed a time of great learning and provided the roundness and grounding to determine how best to tackle life, what works, what doesn't, and why.

It was here that he met and admired so many people but in particular Lynda Pavlik — a woman who knew what she wanted and the shortest route to getting it.

Contents

If you hire the right people, set out clearly what you want them to do, receive confirmation that they can achieve it, provide equipment and training appropriate for them to succeed, establish an environment with like-minded colleagues of freedom to express skills and competencies whilst maintaining strategic direction, gain support for your methods from your peers, your boss and his peers, you are doing what is expected of a people manager.

Introduction

Please read this chapter! People usually avoid reading an introduction. I guess that is because of its title. It gives the impression that this is not the stuff we paid for, that there is better to come, so why bother, let's get at the real stuff.

Perhaps I should have called it *'Cast-iron guarantee to winning the lottery at the first attempt'*.

Well, this introduction does what it says in the title – it introduces you to the simple process of Performance Management – achieving great success from you as a manager of people at any level in an organisation, and from the people who report to you. So you need to read this introduction to get in tune with my thoughts and logic. Besides, it took me ages to write it!

The prompt for writing this book

I believe there is a solution for the almost paranoiac brain-washing type of pressure aimed at us all: to continually adopt the latest business-management fad.

Whilst these fads arguably have their merits, and their time and place, I declare that you don't need them. Or at least not until you can genuinely say that you have a process in place that consistently gets the best results out of every one in the business, that stimulates use of their full range of skills and competencies whilst maintaining strategic business direction.

Then, and only then, should these fads be critically reviewed to determine if they offer some additional benefits to your solid foundation.

Most of these new-fangled fads miss the point about people management. They offer some supposedly new technique or set of tools, with an assumption that you have a solid foundation on which to place them. The ones that relate to people management tend to offer a framework to control the flock rather than get to understand the individuals for whom the people manager has responsibility.

They are promoted as the latest 'must have', the 'not to be seen without' answer to all business performance issues, and are invariably so inflexible that they appear cast in stone.

They provide categories for people at Performance Reviews. You are off track or on track, good or bad, strong or weak, a valued contributor or a major problem.

A psychological nightmare feared by all.

Blame culture

There is usually little argument that people are the main asset to any business. This is generally accepted as a fundamental and valid point.

In reality, in the heat of operating the business, it is often the case that we forget all that and use our people as the labels on which to post our own failings. Our important assets possess identified weaknesses, fail to make the grade, do not reach the standard we expect. True enough, we do have to set standards and we should expect them to be attained. However, there is a step in between setting the standards and measuring results but, because its complexity and time-consuming requirement is not written into the manager's job description, it is mostly glossed over. Time is not allocated to understanding people to get the best out of them. Time has already been allocated to recruiting people. Standards of expectation have been set. Results must happen or else the people have performed poorly or the manager has failed.

Competitive threat disorder

A major requirement of a Performance Management process is for people managers to manage their people by developing an environment for them to express themselves through the free use of their personal skills and competencies – the ones for which they were originally hired.

Regrettably this is not always the case. We humans are prone to *competitive threat disorder* – the fear of one of our people overtaking us, threatening our own position and future prospects.

Tabloid syndrome

We also seem to have an in-built, default, negative attribute – the human enjoyment of shooting people down. The tabloids thrive on it, the TV soaps maintain ratings with it. We enjoy labeling people with critical points in preference to allocating our energies to understanding how to foster and develop the potential of our people through determining and exploiting their strengths.

The message of this book

You don't need the new-fangled fads, buzz words, or today's latest must-have-or-die management techniques, in order to successfully run a modern-day business.

All you need is just plain common sense applied to people and the processes to control their results, with a focus on simplicity, and clarity of understanding.

Make full use of the skills and competencies already inherent in the people employed. Let them go full blast at the objectives you set them, allowing you to measure results against expectations and adjust course accordingly.

The message is:

'Allocate time to understand your people – it will be the best investment you will make.'

It's All You Need!

However, that is not to say that if you adopt the message, everything in the Company garden will be rosy. There are lots of gremlins lurking the corridors of business waiting for an opportunity to screw it all up for you. I refer to some of these in the chapter 'Difficulties and Dangers'.

The book suggests you build your foundation not on the latest fad or buzzword but on common sense, simplicity, and clarity of understanding. From there it is up to you how much you buy-in to the Consultants' patter or the latest must-have from Academialand.

For whom is this book written?

Anyone in the organisation with responsibility for managing people, for getting results in line with strategic direction from the people who report to them.

The book is intended to be generic in that it can be applied to anyone at any time. In the same way, it is not aimed specifically at managers or at individuals. It is intended to be a tool, parts or all of which can be used for any environment which comprises people working together and the processes they adhere to. It applies as equally to the CEO and his direct reports as it does to the despatch manager and his fork-truck drivers.

Style of this book

Having read many management and technical books and talked to other readers of such genres, it is disappointing to find that in order to speed up the learning process, we tend to look to the end of each chapter in the hope of finding a summary that will prevent us having to read the chapter.

This is generally brought about by the writer completing a 700+ page book that feels impressive, looks good on your office shelf and justifies the selling price. Often the chapter content is so deep or technical or – let's be frank here – full of padded garbage, that for anyone reading every word, it would fail to extract the important learning points, unless they hailed from comatosed Academialand.

Thus their chapter summaries are not only important but essential for us to maintain our knowledge of the latest fad, just in case we are asked an awkward question in an open meeting.

The crazy illogic here is that 1,000 books sold at £50 would render £50,000. 50,000 books sold at £6.99 would result in £350,000. So why not write a 150- page book with the waffle cut out? I suspect ego has something to do with this. Dr Bloggs wants to inflate his ego by having his 700pp book recognisable on the family shelf – oh, and the spin-off revenue from speeches, courses and consultations.

The common-sense approach to such management books does not require a title or academic qualifier in front or behind the author's name. That is the whole point! I do not mind being referred to as 'unqualified' or 'no professional qualifications' as long as the message is understood by all, can be applied by anyone, and can really achieve and continue to achieve results.

I have read other books that have clearly been designed with the reader in mind, where the style of writing is so simple with plenty of bullet points, short sections within short paragraphs, with lots of examples and a few line drawings, and a summary to boot. The 'Teach Yourself Books' published by Hodder or the 'in Ninety Minutes' series published by Management Books 2000 spring to mind. You just want to read every word! These are non-complex. For an example of common sense, simplicity, and clarity of understanding applied to a complex subject take a look at any book written by The Motley Fool team on how to invest money.

I have tried to adopt a writing style and layout to make this book readable. I hope it works for you.

Structure of this book

The book is organised in four Parts:

Part 1 – Watch out! They are trying to condition us
Chapter 1: Business Pressures
Chapter 2: A Basic Concept for Success

Part 2 – It's all you need! The main stuff

Part 3 – It's all you need! The other bits

Part 4 – Life is not predictable

Part 1

Watch out! They are trying to condition us

Do you feel the continual pressure that you are a second-rate citizen if you are not up at the leading edge of modern management speak?

1

Business Pressures

Let's take a look at some of the current pressures on us all.

Adopt the latest fad or else!

There is continual pressure put on those who have responsibility for managing people or business processes to adopt the latest fad.

You are not a modern (and therefore acceptable) manager unless you understand and are applying 'Bloggs's Theory of Modern Management for this week'. Oh, and there will be another one along next week, so you had better be ready for that one or you will be left behind and won't be considered for any career development.

The world of management today is all about change. We must change. You must change. What we are changing into today will be obsolete tomorrow. That is the message. Get on the roundabout, or stand there watching the fun go past you.

Well that's all fine and dandy, but let's just call a halt here for a minute and analyse what the real need is.

Let us have a look at the requirements of change. There is sufficient evidence to give support to a need for change. For continual change. An evolution of change as a way of life. No doubt about that whatsoever.

But the media (in the form of consultants, course arrangers, and writers of Academialand management books) would have you believe that what they are offering is part of the deal for necessary change. If you don't take on board the latest fad you will not survive. You will be left so far behind that you will not be able to communicate in the language of the day.

To some degree this is true. But there is change and there is change. This operational management change stuff does not belong in the same camp as changes in legislation, change of technology, change of communications. It would be a very foolish person who ignored the Internet forever. But ignoring Snoggs theory of Management Buzzwords won't actually matter a jot.

You don't need all this radical, revolutionary, new-science stuff dreamed up by the academics and promoted by money-guzzling consultants.

Avoid the hype and go with simple first principles.

The only people who will suffer as a consequence of this attitude and action are:

- the consultants who want to reel you in on their costly fishing line

- the course providers who want to train you in the ways of 'must have to survive'

- the author of the latest fad book, who wants you to read his waffling tome, pretend you understand any of it, and thence promote it as a 'haven't you got a copy yet?'

Change is necessary to keep the mind of both the individual and the organisation active, alert, tested, and ahead of the competition.

Before rushing to embark on this week's special offer promotion for change, consider what is already available to you at no cost and requires no training other than the training of life.

Any of these buzz-worded, highly acclaimed fads are mere *enhancements* to the basic, common-sense management foundation material that is already available to us all. You must have this bolted to the floor, understood and used by all, before embarking on the fads – the good and the less good, the necessary and the less than necessary.

After all, what is wrong with good old common sense? I doubt anyone would argue against it. But surely something else is required besides common sense?

Now, let's try to answer the question, 'Who is pressing for these constant changes?' Well it doesn't take too much searching to see that it mostly comes from the genre of school with names like Bloggs Management Park or Cloggsfield or Snoggs Park Workshop. The very organisations that benefit mostly, if not only, from recommending their kind of change. They are a business and they are therefore out to make money from your attendance.

No doubt they consider the potential attendance and repeat business to be too low for a course titled 'It's all you need!' and whose synopsis highlights common sense, simplicity, and clarity of understanding that we already have in the first place.

They don't really care if you apply all, some, or none of their offerings, as long as they have your money and they can get repeat or on-going business, often on the strength of the prestigious company that has sent you. And whilst they are repeating the same course over again, they are busily safeguarding their future by developing the next 'must-not-be-seen-without' management concept.

I am not for one moment suggesting that applications for training courses should be ripped up or attendance at such courses should be punished by a fate worse than death. Far from it, I firmly believe in picking up any useful tools, hints or tips appropriate to enhance your own area of expertise from whatever source. But it would nice if it were the individual's choice based on a real need rather than the corporate requirement because it feels like the thing to do.

Back in the real world

So having attended Bloggs School of Modern Management Science (BSoMMS) and become a convert (you become either a convert or a sceptic, but they prefer converts!), you head off for the week-end eagerly awaiting the opportunity to put it all into practice first thing on Monday morning.

But what is the reality? Mostly you find that you are unable to implement the newly-acquired learning, because when you arrive at work the following Monday morning, two things happen.

Firstly, you have your 'normal' pre-BSoMMS activities to perform: the ones you are contracted to carry out, that strive for customer satisfaction and ultimately making money. So you will leave it until an opportunity arises. By which time, the impact is watered down along with your memory and enthusiasm for the most important points you want to get across. The best you achieve, because it's natural for people to ask how the course was, is to recommend they all attend.

Secondly, as you enthuse the revelations of the course to everyone you meet – particularly your boss (you have to justify the expense either to him or for him depending on who wanted you to go) – in order to get some buy-in and to set the scene that some new stuff is on its way, you see on their faces the internal groaning that is taking place and you begin to recognise what an up-hill struggle it could be.

You may well find yourself on your own, certainly in a minority, trying to convert the masses. Yet within the BSoMMS course environment it appeared to be nothing more than a formality. After all, you had bought in, so everyone else will. You felt you were the lucky one, they were missing out by not being there to witness this educational experience. You could hardly wait to get back to your people to share your new-found knowledge with them. The course salesman chalked up another disciple.

In the real world of your work domain, it dawns on you that you have a major battle to fight and you may not win unless you can devise a cast-iron motivational strategy.

We love fads really, but ...

This book does not intend to portray a reluctance to condone such elite and well-respected institutions as BSoMMS. It does however, suggest that there is a simple foundation, available to all, to bolt your business to and from which to add knowledge gained from a visit to Academialand.

Yes, there are some excellent new management concepts coming from Academialand and their potential should be reviewed and tested for use within any business. It would be pretty poor management competence not to be up there keeping abreast of what is on offer and interpreting potential opportunities for your business.

But these are enhancements to the basic foundation of common sense, simplicity and clarity of understanding, which must be in place first.

The basic foundation need is for the right people doing the things for which their skills and competencies are appropriately suited within an environment that understands people and promotes their success.

A paradox

Because we employees (yes all of us in the organisation) are objective, focused and to some degree selfish, we naturally are protective of both what we know and where we want to get to. It is a competitive world – dog eat dog. The pressure is there all the time. There is a fear that the achievement of a goal in life may be threatened by a colleague's ability to get there before you if they are armed with the wherewithal to do so. After all, our skills, competencies, and the knowledge and experience gained throughout our lives, are all we have to sell. And while there are the mortgage and utility bills to pay, we have to remain marketable.

Therefore, if you as the manager, provide an environment where your 'competitor' can thrive, grow, add value, it may threaten your marketability and future aspirations with the additional downside of watering-down your control over the rising star.

So there is a natural tendency to suppress potential, to be suspicious, in order to protect your position, to maintain control.

Thus a paradox – the requirement to support growth of our people which itself leads to a resentment of their success for fear of our own security.

In reality, the paradox is invalid. The reverse of the expected results from this natural human fear is actually true. If you let people grow, support them in doing so, grow with them too, allow them to grow beyond you if they are able, then your contribution will be seen as even more valuable.

People management is about getting the best out of people within their sphere of skills, competencies and knowledge.

The very reason a manager fears growth of his or her people is that the manager may be shown lacking in some technical area. But the real people manager is not a technical expert other than in the management of people and any other knowledge acquired along the way. The manager's people have the technical expertise. The manager's expertise is getting the best results from the team he or she is leading.

Until that is understood, in place and operating, the natural human fear of growing colleagues remains to stifle growth of the business.

Take a wider view

We humans tend to be so short-sighted that we focus on the short term, what is going on in front of us today and tomorrow, but with less regard for the big picture of life, the full width of opportunity.

We let our fears build up out of this immediate environment, because that is the tangible one – it is there for us to live and breathe today, right now. Anything else is speculation, potential, the future, unreal.

Most people move between companies sometime in their working lives. Very few people remain in the same job. Those that do will usually move around, if not physically then within changing job requirements as the business meets changing market needs.

It is currently between two and four years that a job change occurs in some way or other.

So what is a desperately feared competitive issue today will be forgotten when the manager or the 'competitor' has moved on, lost forever to the memory following a change of job. It was only important when the 'competition' was seen by you to threaten your position.

Yet strangely, encouraging your people to grow, even past you, will remain in the memory. Those events are not forgotten. They remain as if a deliberate reward for being bold, to assist you later in overcoming the fear of competition, and give you the ability to deal positively with competition.

I had responsibility for a software engineer a few years back who was hired to assist my team to develop an electronic publishing system. The guy was good and soon, through his dedicated effort and sheer hard work, became not just a local expert but the source for technical solutions from all round the international company we worked for at that time.

He was critical to our development but also valuable around the world – there being only a handful of his kind anywhere. Had I stifled him, the group would have failed to develop the product and I would have lost my key player.

Originally hired at a level below me I had to support his rise to two levels above me. It did hurt, it didn't seem right that I had supported this guy through the development of a product that was fuelling his ability to command great wealth from life.

The product was completed successfully and to time. The guy moved to the US and has gone on to even greater things. He deserves the best.

That was my learning, about how not to fear people who have opportunities you may not have, and it focused me on my role in life.

I have never forgotten it, and it has served me well since.

A word about change

The word 'change' is one of the most frequently used in modern-day business speak. It is a word that creates enormous pressure on people right across organisations. It promotes fear of the unknown, paints a picture of threat to the comfort zones, and does not readily enlist support. Yet it is completely the wrong word for the intended meaning.

Change is a state of being, not a result or a benefit.

'Enhancement' is a more appropriate word but doesn't have the same ring or implied force as 'change'.

But it does imply a benefit, a benefit on top of something already good.

Change implies that something is wrong and thus there is a need to correct it by throwing everything out of the window and starting again – until the next change, which indicates a cycle and sets an expectation that there will always be another change, so what's the point of taking this one too seriously?

That is exactly the way most people have come to recognise change. It has become the bad news, the negative option, and an implied criticism of everyone who has supported the current modus operandi. Additionally, it is seen as yet another management initiative – one that we will have to go along with until the next one comes along – and how much did this one cost us?

Stop using the word 'change' and start using a more appropriate word such as 'enhancement'.

Even when you do have to tear up the operating manual and go back to the drawing board, it remains an enhancement – you must have been doing something right (perhaps other factors have created a different environment) so it is a change of direction which itself is an enhancement.

However, it has to be an enhancement to a solid foundation that is already yielding benefits from the basic attributes of the organisation.

Back to common sense

If people are our most important asset, then it is upon them that managers should focus their attention.

Rather than impose on them the latest buzz-worded fad and switching them off, invest time to understand this most important asset and see what is already available from within them.

Look no further than a Performance Management process.

Summary of Opportunities

- You don't have to buy the hype – be selective, choose and interpret the potential of fads on offer, for your environment.

- Build the foundation on first principles – fads can come later.

- Fear not the competition from within – use their strengths to enhance your own position.

- Take a wider view – be bold, try the unknown, put on the varifocals.

- Be clear what is meant by change, and what you mean by your change. Stop using the word 'change' – find a better word.

- Cultivate your most important asset.

- Performance Management will cost you nothing but earn you great wealth.

You have a choice.

You choose the complexity of leading edge management buzz-words and fads to control the destiny of your business. Your focus thus becomes keeping yourself up-to-date whilst watching the ever-widening gulf appear between you and your bemused people.

You had the option to choose common sense, simplicity, and clarity of understanding as a foundation for control.

You want to try it again?

2

A Basic Concept for Success

Fear not avoiding the hype!
There is an alternative.

It's all you need!

A Performance Management process comprises two parts:

- a process to manage the performance of people

- a process to monitor progress, audit results measured against plan, and take action if necessary to maintain strategic direction.

This process with its two parts can help us solve the whole damn messy equation of our working lives.

What we are looking at is an effective process to manage the people of the business and a process to evaluate its results and take any remedial action to maintain our direction in line with the business plan. You can even use it outside of the work environment, but work is the one we are concerned with, so that is the one on which we focus here.

Applying our principles of common sense, simplicity and clarity of understanding, we can test the validity.

It has to be **Common Sense** to focus on people and relate their inherent contribution to desired business results.

With just two parts to control the business, it certainly satisfies the principle of **Keep It Simple**. Why make a process more complicated than it needs to be?

Clarity of understanding is more easily achieved by having fewer things to focus on – there are just two: *People* and a *Results Information Service*. Being honest with people about what you want, and determining what they can realistically achieve, makes for a pretty clear situation. Regular progress reporting and open communications provides an opportunity to make things crystal clear and reduces the opportunity for surprise set-backs.

The two parts are complimentary. Focusing on people, and their contribution, sharing results of their efforts and dealing with issues as they arise, all leads to increased motivation, ownership, and trust.

Let your people know what you want

The Performance Management process provides you the opportunity to let your people know in clear terms precisely what you want them to do and what is expected of them.

The objectives set by your manager for you to achieve should be a reflection of some part of the strategic business direction.

The objectives you set your people will be an interpretation of your own objectives translated into local requirements.

By setting clear objectives for each of your people, that can be traced back to your own objectives and to the strategy of the business, you are assured your team is rowing in the right direction and is doing its part. So too are you.

You are also demonstrating your understanding of the strategic direction the business is taking and sharing ownership of achievement with your people.

However, by taking it one step further, you will enhance your genuine understanding of the objectives and display a sense of ownership and sharing with your people in how each objective can be achieved.

This part of the process is the setting of Measurable Tasks that relate to each objective. There can be as many as you like, but each task must …

- be measurable in some demonstrable way
- relate to its objective
- be achievable.

… and the combined success of each task should determine the achievement of the objective.

The objective says what is to be achieved and the tasks determine how it will be achieved.

Seek agreement

Setting the objectives that you want and agreeing with your people that they can be achieved, will achieve far more than imposing objectives and walking away.

In order to expand each objective into Measurable Tasks you will naturally determine the logical route to successful achievement of the objective. You will demonstrate to your people that you understand that each objective is actually achievable and not just desirable, an aspiration.

By working with them to determine reasonable Measurable Tasks, obstacles and issues and concerns will arise related to the working environment, such as equipment and training needs.

Addressing these fosters genuine ownership of desire to achieve success, and provides the best environment for the next stage.

Let them get on with it

Whilst you as the manager must be utterly committed to the success of your people in achieving their objectives, you must allow them the freedom to get on with their jobs. This is the requirement. They have the skills. They will bring you success. You are not there to do it for them. Your role is to be there for them in times of conflict, to assist in dealing with issues and concerns, to decide direction, to make judgement calls, and report progress, whilst focusing on developing the strategy of your part of the business.

Your people need to know that you are aware of their efforts and of their striving for success through all the difficulties they encounter.

But you are not there to do their job for them. The business has hired good people with the right skills and competencies.

The biggest trap a manager can fall into is to fail to recognise this and to carry out the requirements of the role of the people hired to do it. Getting sucked into doing the job of your people is fraught with obvious disasters. It is an easy situation in which to find yourself and a difficult one from which to get out. You will sink and be less effective as their manager and they will sit back and do less. You will have no one but yourself to blame. You, as manager are the driver, you determine the road down which to travel.

Detaching yourself too much will lead to your people feeling misunderstood, uncared for, the troops in the trenches, pawns in the game. But it is so easy either to do the job for them or become too detached. If you try to do their jobs you run a risk of stifling their flair, personal development, and team development. If you detach yourself it will be seen as lacking ownership, commitment and team leadership.

The real skill here is to keep to the middle ground with good use of flexibility. You are there to direct, to maximise use of their skills and competencies, for the benefit of the business.

Let your people get on with their tasks whilst promoting an awareness that you are there and tuned in to what is going on.

It is a fine line and must be watched constantly.

Control or anarchy?

There must however be some form of controls that ensure corporate etiquette is applied or else ego anarchy will prevail resulting in the sound of packs of tumbling cards.

For example, there may be business principles in effect to which anything and everything must take note and abide by accordingly.

There may also be a Quality System in place such as ISO9000.

This will require such procedures as Contract Review to be incorporated into objectives for those people who have responsibility for accepting customer orders.

This is not to say that by controlling the process, the people are restricted in applying their individual flair and developing ideas. Far from it, any business today will only continue to be successful if through on-going development, it ensures it is not standing still and neither are its people.

Develop your people

Developing the people will ensure that the business development roundabout is already spinning. But the people must be developed at a pace that achieves the best results. All of us are different, we develop at different rates, we assimilate knowledge at differing rates. In order to gain the highest development results from our people, they must firstly be understood. What makes them tick?

So often this aspect is ignored or lip service is paid to it. If an individual is slow to grasp the issues, if he can't keep up, if he is unable to go at the pace of the manager, then he is placed on a lower rung on the ladder of valued contribution to the business.

Generally, people managers do not allot themselves time to evaluate the complexity of their people, and are not supported in that activity by their bosses. If one individual is not performing to expectations, that is their problem and it's too bad. Everybody else has grasped what to do.

Many managers set their people objectives and expectations based on their own ability, capability, pace, speed, mental agility, skills and competencies. They expect their people to be clones of themselves and find it difficult to tolerate performances that do not reflect their own. There is a long way to go for these people to be People Managers.

Development must be on-going within the business – that in itself is an activity, or set of activities that needs to be controlled along with the business's normal activities.

Results information service

Having let your people get on with their jobs, you need to be assured that all is well.

For this you need two kinds of information:

- progress reports
- business results data.

Progress reports, in the form of Project Report, Monthly Report, or whatever is deemed to be appropriate, will come from your people because you will have set this as one of their task activities.

Objective:	Provide periodic information reports to ensure your manager is fully aware of success and failure, plans and revisions, and areas needing help and support.
Measurable Task:	Report monthly, progress on each project.
Measurable Task:	Provide a Monthly Report no greater than 1 side A4, reporting: achievements this month planned actions for next month issues and concerns.
Measurable Task:	Monthly Report to be emailed to manager by end of day 3 of month following.

Business results data should be provided by whatever system is in place either through your own level of authority or through a request to other departments or personnel who have the information you need.

Progress reports and business data provide you with the opportunity to measure current results against plan and make any course changes appropriate to maintain the planned direction.

Shaping the future

If you are now operating as the model People Performance Manager, you have secured time to devote to developing the future strategy of the business as applied to your corner of its society.

It's all you need

With the foundation process of Performance Management firmly in place and supported by a Results Information Service, anything else becomes subordinate to these two, or invokes Clause 99 (see later on).

Summary of Opportunities

- Manage the People and the data from the Results Information Service.

- Be clear what you want your people to do.

- Make sure their objectives are achievable, and linked to your own objectives.

- Break objectives into measurable tasks.

- Give your people freedom to get on with it.

- Determine controls to prevent ego anarchy without stifling flair.

- You need results information.

- Understand what makes your people tick.

- Develop the people and the business will develop itself.

Part 2

It's All You Need!
– the Main Stuff

Far better to give people
their freedom to express
themselves, to use their
personal skills and
competencies to the full,
at their own effective pace,
than to stand over them and
tell them what to do.

3

Understand People

What makes us tick?

We are complex beings

Humans are certainly complex. It would be difficult enough to understand our complexity if we all acted in a similar manner in any given circumstance. But we don't. It's impossible. We are not robots. It is difficult to predict our actions with certainty every time. We programme our responses according to a whole raft of emotive forces such as our mood, how we currently feel about the people around us, our sense of well-being, home circumstances, work issues, finance, health and so on. The list is endless and any one thing can and does affect our predictability.

Additionally, we each have our individual traits, our personal needs, and our modus operandi, which we continue to develop throughout our lifetimes, and which will be impacted by the various circumstances in which we find ourselves at any particular time.

No, we are not predictable. Even those of us who repeat their actions time and time again in the same manner will unexpectedly do it a different way at some point in time.

So trying to understand us is a major task. Our complexity is the reason psychologists exist. The good people manager has to be part psychologist. In order to get the best out of people he or she must understand them, understand what makes them tick, gives them a buzz, upsets them, makes them perform well consistently, and what is likely to make their performance tail off.

Being a people manager is a tough job and mostly misunderstood. The manager is often criticised amongst his subordinates (and sometimes openly) along the lines, 'Why do we need you? What do you actually do?' In times of financial difficulty the people manager may be regarded as expendable and added to the head count reduction to save costs. The people manager's success is mostly hidden from view. He assists his people in being successful but it can be them that are seen to be invaluable.

The goal is, of course, to get the best out of people. This requires an understanding of their potential and the provision of an environment that will turn that potential into a reality, without being seen to pander to their needs. It is a fine line and it is nothing but hard work and perseverance that will reap its own reward.

People and their comfort zones

The traditional, if not natural, human instinct is to look for the area of most comfort whilst expending the least amount of effort. Without going into the theory of evolution, it would be hard for anyone to disagree that it is not just humans.

I am sure, if it only could, the domestic cat would live in a tree house close to the birds and have it fully insulated so that it could sleep warmly in peace and quiet, only taking a break to stretch a paw outside to catch lunch. The mighty lion in the jungle does as little as possible other than sleep, have sex, and eat what the lioness has caught. We all like our comfort zone and resent pressure to move outside it. We also, like the lion, are happy to do the job that's required and no more.

However, each of us has a differing definition of comfort zone.

The workaholic may find comfort in work, but will still look to expend the least effort to achieve a goal.

The perceived 'lazybones' will look to avoid additional work, to extend their tasks, to add that bit more, preferring to exploit the sympathy or naivety of others to make up for their own inefficiency.

The job of people manager is all the more difficult because the people manager has a comfort zone too.

The complexity is further extended if the people manger tries to test the validity of Lazy Bones.

Lazy Bones could be inefficient because he or she is:

- in need of motivation
- looking for a raison d'etre
- desperate for recognition of potential
- depressed by being undervalued
- disillusioned from failed promises
- just not up to the job into which they have been 'reorganised'
- a natural lazy bones
- a triangular peg in a hexagonal hole
- a whole host of other reasons.

Both workaholic and lazybones have their reasons for the way they operate which the people manager should try to understand if he or she wants to get the best out of them.

People and the need to be managed

Undoubtedly people will give of their best in an environment that gives them the freedom to express themselves and demonstrate their skills and competencies to the full, at their own pace.

People (other than when training) need direction more than they need close supervision. Giving direction is far better than telling them what to do. The rewards for both parties will be all the greater.

But first you must channel effort into trying to understand people – and this must be a continuing exercise.

In understanding each of his or her people, trying to channel them into areas of best fit, and providing an environment of freedom for them to operate, the people manager must provide direction in order that his or her area is synchronised with the wider aims of the business as a whole.

In the modern business world with its prominent requirement of 'compete or be gone', the need for people to be managed continues in order to maintain pulse rate, focus on achieving the objective, and do that little bit more, to be comfortably stretched.

The combination of freedom of expression and firm but clear direction are prerequisites to competitive success.

The emphasis may have moved toward self-management but the requirement for people management is just as strong today as ever. Left to their own devices, humans soon lose the plot.

If an army is not led it will not initiate a battle. It will wait for commands from a leader. Without its people manager, it has no direction, no game plan. It is likely not to train and will eventually lose its purpose, form splinter groups and be less effective, if not useless in the event of the need to fight or be a force to be reckoned with. Look at the difference between a European army and a third-world army.

Closer to home, ask yourself the searching question, 'If your boss doesn't come in today, do you work as hard and for how long do you maintain the same pace?'

How do you work when your boss is on holiday? Be honest now! What is your work ethic if you learn that he or she was going to be off for three weeks unexpectedly and there will be no temporary replacement?

So we humans mostly need a pilot to fly our craft in the direction set by the Chief of Command, and in accordance with procedures in the Flight Manual.

I'll tell you what to do!

Here lies a paradox. We need someone to tell us what to do but we resent being told what to do!

Thus there is a need for some techniques and tools that fool the human mind into accepting instructions, commands, change (oh! that awful and misused word 'change'!) etc, willingly, with enthusiasm, buy-in, and with contribution. Is 'buy-in' a buzz word? Ok, how about support and commitment?

It is all about the style of the request. It has little to do with intellect, intelligence, or skills and competencies – unless your boss is masochistic and you are a sadist you are not likely to agree to something that is certain to fail. It does have everything to do with the natural way the human mind works and our natural need for recognition and appreciation.

In the example of your boss being on holiday, if he said to you before leaving, 'Keep the ship running whilst I am away, oh, and I would be over the moon if you could manage to complete XYZ task ready for you and I to review when I return'. Now, even if it is a slim chance, even if it involves significant additional effort on your part, you will be inspired and focused to achieve a result. A good result too. We all need recognition and appreciation in varying degrees.

Remember too that your boss cannot be successful unless you and your colleagues are successful. Therefore your boss must get the best out of you.

A word about leadership

The dictionary definition of leadership says, 'The capacity to lead others along a way; to give guidance'. However, if the leader just stands on the mountain and paints the vision and the direction in which to go, there would be no assurance that the message would be understood. It may not be heard at all or it may be misinterpreted. The manager must know that his direction is well understood, that he is aware of subsequent progress, and aware of anything hindering that progress.

The manager is as much part of the team as are the people. But there can be only one leader. There must be only one clear message.

The manager needs to know if he is communicating, i.e. is the message clear, and understood. Was it the right one for the objective to be achieved? Is there ever a right one? How do you know how effective it is? It may be effective but still upset significant numbers of people. So is that really effective?

Whilst maintaining a position of authority, the manager will be wise to seek to understand that his or her people understand the message and are fully on board. That gives the greatest opportunity for success.

Here is an example of questionable dual-direction communication flow.

Ask a supermarket checkout girl at if she is happy and she will respond in the affirmative, especially with a queue of customers and the supervisor within earshot. But ask her when she has more time to talk and there are no other people around, least of all her Supervisor and you will receive a tale of woe – 'I don't know why I work here, they haven't got a clue, nobody knows what is going on, nobody listens to me.'

Yet the supervisor probably thinks communicating is working okay and if it isn't working, well then, it's the checkout girl who isn't up to the job.

Ask the top managers in the supermarket's HQ how their workers are and they will give a glowing response littered with statistics, data, graphs, and feedback from employee surveys.

The legitimate claims and the equally important improvement ideas, from shelf fillers and check-out staff often appear to fall on deaf ears or are noted out of sympathy but not recorded and not progressed.

I am not for one minute suggesting that every claim they have should result in giving them what they want, or that every improvement idea could be turned into practical success. But it is often the case that claims and ideas are not recorded and responded to. Thus with no movement up the chain of command, the top-level managers assume that everything is wonderful in the kitchen. This chain had some seriously shattered links. There should be a process to log the claims and ideas, determine action and communicate what that action is including impact in terms of cost and efficiency so that it can be measured later to see if it was actually justified. Rejected claims and ideas should equally be recorded and fed back along with reasons. That is not only common sense but plain courtesy.

An understanding, a fact-finding and further investigation process, is inexpensive to operate, yet yields big rewards in employee satisfaction when a solution is implemented.

In the recent TV documentary series 'Back to the Floor', when the top people at HQ donned overalls and entered one of their shops on shelf-filling duty, or the bakery at 3am or the hotel concierge's room just as the coach party was arriving, they were alarmed to find that what they were hearing in reports was more than a little way off from reality.

So were they good leaders? Certainly not from the view point of 'Is my message getting through, am I aware of progress and any stumbling blocks impeding progress'.

A side step to improvement ideas

I firmly believe in a phrase that was drummed into me many years ago by my American boss at that time, 'Always look for a better way to do business'. She was so right about that. Any business, in order to survive in the competitive market place, cannot stand still. It must frequently improve its processes to remain competitive. The minute it stops, the time when complacency arrives, is the time that business starts to die.

I don't necessarily go along with the obsessional 'continuous improvement' process as drummed into businesses by over-dramatic consultants. It can shift the focus away from core business activities because the consultants left behind a process and convinced the business that continuous improvement meant completing that process fully and completely. Consultants' processes are rarely interpreted at board level, rather passed down the line to be followed to the letter. If you were to contemplate interpretation, then you would come up with the process in the first place and not need consultants!

However, to review everything that is done, frequently and by the people who do it, must – absolutely must – be a part of business doctrine. Once it becomes a default way of life, the improvements will come and the benefits realised. It does not always have to be huge quality improvement teams who are assigned to monthly meetings in the quest for improvements, resulting in masses of reports and creating fear in team members if they fail to improve anything. It does need to be a way of thinking whilst working.

I recall a company that included improvement ideas in its monthly reporting process up to board level. Not a bad thing to do – maintaining awareness of what is happening down the chain. However, the board became so obsessed with their desire for improvements that it actually budgeted for a number per month and raised serious questions with functional managers when targets were not achieved. This resulted in ridiculous ideas being put forward out of fear.

Far better for the board to identify less profitable areas within the business and push down to functional teams specific requests for improvement ideas.

It should be a natural occurrence at functional level between a manager and his team to always look for a better way to do business. The board will see the fruit of this soon enough in the business results.

Managers have a role to play here to encourage the adoption of a default continuous improvement way of life amongst their people.

People manager expectations

So what is expected of the people manager?

Well, of course it will be different in every company and within industries, and it will certainly be different vertically in the organisation too. Although people managers can vary their roles operationally from the 'One-Minute Manager' type to the hands-on-and-very-much-involved-in-everything type.

But fundamentally the job of every manager can be summarised (albeit very simply) in the following points:

1. Being there when your people need you. Directing, chairing, motivating, visioning, and giving guidance and support. Monitoring progress of Objectives and their effect on the business.

2. Owning a development plan for each of your people.

3. Carrying out specific routine tasks such as reporting progress up and down the chain of command, the analysis of output results, revising the strategic plan, attending meetings

3. Developing and implementing strategy at whatever level exposed to – taking the business forward.

4. Taking responsibility for, and ownership of, the functional area assigned (people, process, environment, equipment, output, performance, etc). Being accountable for its success and its failings.

Often, managers consider objectives to be achieved as a default expectation because the manager set the objectives in accordance with the requirements set on him by his or her boss – generally a one-sided affair – *'This is what I want you to do, so just get on and do it!' 'What do you mean you expect support from me? Of course you will get my support – I am just rather busy right now, er ... do what you can. But you do have my whole-hearted backing (I hope she doesn't expect me to get involved).'*

If you screw up, you are less of a valued contributor – with little consideration for the difficulties involved or most importantly the relationships required with colleagues in order to achieve individual success.

There are very few people managers – real people managers. A lot think they are if for no other reason because they are assigned a responsibility for a bunch of people and therefore by default they are a people manager. Because they are reasonably good at their job (however they choose to go about getting results) they are able to justify considering themselves good people managers.

Yet the reality is that there are few real people managers. Nowhere near as many as there should be. Yet there are thousands of managers, assigned responsibility for people, out there in industries.

With top-notch, effective people managers, businesses achieve more because the people contribute more, and by working more effectively rather than being over-tasked by their pressured manager.

They own their responsibility having agreed the size of their work tasks.

Less-than-good people management arises from fear, pressure, naivety and lack of care and consideration.

- There may be **fear of failure** on the part of the manager. He can cover himself by having a name to put in the frame if failure does occur, i.e. the manager needs to have somebody to 'blame' for his team's failure – and it needs to be somebody else but the manager. *'I just don't know what he was doing. I really didn't expect such poor performance. I gave him clear instructions and he nodded enthusiastically, I didn't expect to have to stand over him all day. I expected better. I'll have a word.'*

- There may be **pressure from the organisation** to get results, to achieve, and to do it fast. There is little tolerance within business organisations for understanding people. *'Why should that be necessary? People are hired to achieve.'* There is an expectation that they will because they are being paid to achieve. They are considered numbers, expendable numbers – there is always another one waiting to take your place. So, people are used in the game of trying to run a business to be successful.

- There may be a **lack of company support** for understanding its people. People are hired to do a job, whatever it might be re-engineered to be and they are paid well to do it. The organisation allocates little time to understanding individuals so as to know their strengths and their limitations and where to employ them to extract the best of those qualities they offer. It doesn't consider that to be a necessarily fruitful exercise. How often have people been promoted to positions of 'incompetence' for convenience?

People managers have a tough challenge. They have a responsibility to their bosses and their companies to achieve the results they have committed to. Those results can only be achieved through the performance of the people reporting to them. They have a responsibility to their people to ensure they have the right direction and environment in which to successfully complete tasks that enable objectives to be achieved. They may well have to fight in both directions at different times in order to fulfil their responsibilities.

A word about 'weakness' – an unnecessary evil

Weakness is one of those words used by default in off-the-shelf Performance Management systems. These will always contain a section on 'Strengths and weaknesses'.

Why, oh why, should weaknesses be attributed to individuals. In reality, people hired through a formal recruitment process don't have weaknesses. They have levels of potential contribution associated with the skills and competencies they bring to the organisation. There are Go and No-Go areas, strengths and limitations, but there are no weaknesses unless an individual has deliberately been deceitful at interview or on his or her CV or there is some external pressure affecting their performance which results in a weak (less than expected) performance from an otherwise good performer.

However, if a technically competent individual, who does not have a natural affinity for figures, is promoted to a position with responsibility for forecasting profit in his section and reports less well than a figure-happy colleague, it is seen as a 'weakness'. If financial training is then provided for this technocrat and subsequent results are little better it is seen as a serious weakness! The business has now invested money in training this person and the investment is not seen to have paid off. No doubt the manager will have justified the training investment too, so this result reflects badly on him.

The truth is that it is a management responsibility in the first place to make the judgement that this promotion can work, that the employee can continue to be successful through support and training. To continue to turn in that valued contribution that led to the promotion in the first place.

But whilst the manager owns responsibility for the suitability of the individual to cope with tasks assigned, the individual has a part to play too. He has the opportunity to voice his concern about his competence limitations in this case with matters financial. However, frequently a promotion will be readily accepted regardless of ability as, unlike buses, they rarely come along in threes and the increase in salary will go a long way to paying for the new extension to the kitchen.

It is short-sighted for all parties to allow this situation to happen. The next Performance Review will highlight the need for training to help with the identified 'weakness'. The individual will be required to attend a relevant training course to help overcome the 'weakness'. Worse still, HR or the Training Officer will have been asked to search their databanks for a course suitable for this person's 'problem'. The employee has acquired a record! The previously valued contributor who was recommended for promotion has now acquired a record of questionable performance.

In performance measurement terms, this is a correct mechanical process. But should the individual have been put in that position in the first place? When considered for promotion, where was the process to review his potential contribution to the organisation?

If reviewed effectively, one of two conclusions would have been drawn.

● There is potential for this individual to become effective with figures through training, a development plan, and an assigned mentor who is accountable for managing the plan.

● This individual will always struggle (at this point in time) to be comfortable with figures – his understanding may improve as may his contribution regarding figures, but he is unlikely to be a top performer in this particular aspect of his new role. Therefore we must accept that and ensure that we, as a responsible employer, do not pressure this valued employee with tasks unrelated to his strengths.

It is not criticism – how can it be? It is *fact*. If it is considered a weakness, then the business has failed and is definitely incorrect in its conduct. The business promotes a valued contributor, then documents their 'weaknesses' and its consequential failings!

Development need

There is a complimentary problem with the term 'weakness' and that is 'development need'. But first it is worth looking at how these terms managed to become common business usage.

They came about through the application of the Consultant's 'framework for people management' and the like. Organisations tend to buy the ready-made people management framework off the shelf by parting with vast (and they are vast) sums of money. This framework and its associated manuals and training courses on how to make use of them (and additional vast sums) will include sections which deal with either 'weaknesses' or 'development needs'. I can hear the chair creaking as you squirm.

We have already looked at 'weaknesses'. It should not be applied to any individual unless, perhaps, just maybe, in a situation of severe discipline.

'Development needs' however, is something to embrace warmly and apply when evaluating peoples' strengths. Yes, their *strengths*. It is an opportunity to further enhance their valued contribution without putting them into potential failure mode! If this opportunity proves to be fruitful – to be able to develop their strengths further – the value of this employee's contribution will be enhanced. It must be – fact. The worth of this employee to the organisation will be high.

If you have recruited the right people, they will all be good, valued contributors. Some will have higher values than others, but they will all be good and they will all be valued contributors.

There will be areas in which they will not be competent and may not ever be able to be competent. These are not weaknesses, they are no-go areas. Focus on the strengths alone. Develop the strengths if possible. If not, leave alone – with no criticism.

Unfortunately, the consultants' framework invariably includes a section on 'dealing with weaknesses' and 'development needs arising from identified weaknesses' – and the training course the consultant provides will allocate time to weaknesses and development needs. Thus the organisation will automatically include an expectation that every appraisal will contain some words defining every employee's weaknesses and/or their development needs arising therefrom.

Typically, there will be a box for the appraisee and one for the appraiser which will be headed 'List 5 weaknesses identified during the appraisal citing evidence where possible'.

Yeah, like let's all focus on what you can't do. Let's rack our brains until we come up with five nice and juicy things you are really crap at, and then let's make you feel really good about it by writing them down and sending copies to your boss and to HR! Why not put one on the notice board?

What a waste of time! Let common sense prevail here! Develop the strengths – there is a return to be made on your investment. What sort of return can ever be made by focusing effort on managing a weakness derived from lack of natural competence?

Morale will take a dive. Even the training officer, who initially will feel motivated by job security with the enormity of the training need, will become demotivated through course feedback and insignificant change to employee weakness level. Course feedback will talk of 'It did nothing for me' and 'I found it a complete waste of my time' and 'Why was I singled out for this course?'

Of course, this doesn't mean we are so perfect that we don't need help from time to time – and maybe at times when we can't see a problem ourselves. We are human and we are vulnerable. We do have weak spots within our strength potential.

Any manager worth his or her salt will identify development needs during the year and put in place plans to help improve people so that when reviewed, a developing strength will be recorded. Any managers who document a weakness other than under a disciplinary heading, are guilty of admitting their own failure to identify a development need and to take some corrective action as a matter of course and well before the appraisal.

It may be worth, at this point, using an example to reaffirm the distinction between 'weakness' and genuine 'development need'.

A manager determines through a people performance measurement process that one of his charges would be more effective as a result of time-management training. This is not a weakness. It is the development of a strength. Yet it may be seen by the employee that the manager has identified a weakness because the employee (until they have received training) will not readily see that there is an efficiency advantage to be gained both by the organisation and by the employee. The subject must therefore be handled with care and tact.

Additionally, there may be an instance when an individual wishes to change direction, or at least to test a change of direction, and will request assistance with this development need. For example, a senior manager may aspire to a position of General Manager but has little accountable experience for matters financial. The senior manager may be competent with figures and with reading and understanding P&L Statements and Balance Sheets, and have been involved with budget preparation, but her current job has not provided an environment for her to take responsibility or make judgements, let alone be accountable, for such activities. This is a development need – not a weakness – and if the senior manager has requested training, it should be fully embraced and endorsed. Yet often it will be seen as unnecessary, or privately feared as being competitive. What if the person is good at it? Will that threaten the position of potential peer general managers in the organisation?

If someone is offered a trial run and finds it tough and unsuitable at this time, it is often seen as a failure. Yet the reality is that the employee:

- put their hand in the air and had a go
- sent a clear message requesting greater responsibility or a new challenge
- has gained knowledge and experience during the trial process
- will always retain that knowledge and experience
- will be better able to understand the business from whichever position they occupy
- should be considered for the position, or a similar one, at a later point in time.

The addition of human complexity

Every human being's needs will be different. From the workaholic who operates like the work sponge to the more ethical 'you pay me for 8 hours I give you 8 hours' eye-for-an-eye approach.

Whichever way, humans are so complex that it is impossible to know our makeup, what motivates us, what environment we will operate in more effectively. We don't always say what we would like to say – for fear of admitting failure or inability.

The surface manager will miss (or doesn't care about) the reality when his team member, in response to *'I want you to take on this objective'* says *'no problem!'* Under review, the manager will say *'I don't understand what happened, he said he could do it, he was very positive about it'*. The reality is that the individual was probably cringing inside and thinking : Oh God, how am I going to do this? but unprepared to admit it for fear that his boss might say *'Oh, really, you are not comfortable with this, er ... well ... maybe I should review the conditions of your promotion and where you can go from here because obviously this limits you'*. How stupid we are. Your boss is not going to do that, but we tend to consider that it might happen – or that admitting a lack of competence in some area of our new portfolio will be not only viewed as the dreaded 'weakness' but documented as such, talked about, and discussed behind closed HR doors.

This is where the complexity becomes greater. In the ideal organisation, HR would tactfully assist the manager in ways of understanding the team member and to recognise and play to given strengths and develop areas of expertise unfamiliar to him or her. However, the quality of HR will now play a part and ultimately affect the team member. Not just the quality of the HR advisors – their performance in this matter may well be influenced by their boss or the style of performance requirement instilled by the organisation itself.

Managers can find themselves operating under that natural human trait – most comfort from least effort.

And what of the expectations of the poor individual at the bottom of the pile – the team member who is oblivious to all this closed, and yet so open, awareness that there is a 'weakness'. There is, of course, a weakness – a real one – but it doesn't lie with the team member. It lies with the process.

So here lies the rub. The organisation needs a robust People Performance process, yet the very process will be as effective as the quality of the people who operate it. There is no Utopia. That can never be achieved. We are human, we are different, the variety of ingredients that go to make the human cake will always yield varied and unpredictable products from the bakery.

But as an individual you can strive to do your bit as effectively as you can. That (along with encouraging others) is the best you can do to maximise employee potential.

You owe that to the people reporting to you. And to improve yourself if you can see your colleagues are getting better results. You too have to be honest and have the courage to ask the good people manager for some insight and help to enhance your strength

Everyone has a bad hair day once in a while

Even good performers have their off days. We are only human! It is unrealistic to expect even the best contributors to perform at the highest level every minute of every day. It just does not happen. Our lives are complex. We introduce ingredients that affect our performance. The World Cup quarter final is showing on the big screen in your local at midnight tonight. Your seat is booked, the beer flows. Your performance the morning after will be directly related to the amount of alcohol consumed and influenced by the result of the game.

The human body is full of clocks and rhythms that look after our wellbeing and regulate our body parts according to conditions. Biorhythms are said to affect certain elements in our make up. These are the rhythms that commence their cycle at the point of birth and continue to have positive and negative effects on our emotional, physical, and intellectual state throughout our lives. The rhythms are said to have different cycle lengths – 28, 33, 23 days – and when key points in the cycles coincide we can perform almost out of character

– sometimes better, sometimes less well. We can perform mental or physical tasks more easily or make uncharacteristic mistakes.

You may well pooh-pooh biorhythms but one international airline takes them so seriously that they will not allow their pilots to fly in the days surrounding one of these critical points. The airline considers the risk to passengers, through making a wrong decision at 36,000 feet, too great.

People and the need to do a bit more

It is a natural human trait in the majority of cases to keep the status quo rather than develop the process. This is not to be confused with being shown some new tool that can make the existing process easier to manage. That falls into the same category as 'comfortable' and is therefore willingly accepted (although there may be some initial suspicion until proof is obtained).

To venture into the unknown, to try something new, to embark on development where there might come a point where the option to return to comfortland is lost to you – that is reserved for the foolhardy, the adventurous, the entrepreneur, the other guy.

But take some time to consider what motivates you to do this little bit extra. Your salary will not increase directly upon your boss's return from the South of France when you have done that extra task he hinted at. You will not be instantly promoted as a consequence. You don't actually have to do it.

What you are looking for is another aspect of human need. Some praise, a recognition, a sense of value, of being valued, of being wanted, part of the team, somebody who can be relied upon.

In short, a valued contributor.

Sure, you may well consider a link here with promotion and salary increases, but it's not the precise reason for your completing the task enthusiastically and well. We have a natural need for appreciation for a job well done. That includes self-appreciation too.

However, you should also be motivated by a genuine concern as to what happens to the business if you don't do that little extra, go the extra mile, examine potential, ask the question 'why?'

Every company must renew itself, refresh its parts, alter its shape through experimentation and strategic development, in order for it to remain at the front in the competitive market place – to lead, more than to compete.

The best-selling book *'Who Moved My Cheese?'* says it all. I sometimes wonder how this type of book becomes a best seller when its content is obvious, so simply written as to be patronising, makes few pages and takes 17 minutes to read from beginning to end. Yet it, along with *The One Minute Manager* and the like, do become best sellers because they have a common-sense message, albeit idealistic, and they say it all. Perhaps they become best sellers because readers recognise the idealism as something to aspire to, which is a good thing providing that aspiration is maintained and turned into a plan of action.

Summary of Opportunities

- Get your people out of their comfort zones!

- Give your people a realistic, clear brief and an appropriate working environment for them to achieve.

- Give them direction but let them manage themselves.

- Be there! Provide realistic and continued support.

- Push the envelope.

- Drop the ego – there's no long-term benefit in telling people how to do their jobs, or expecting them to do it exactly as you do – you will most likely learn something from their way.

- They need to know what you expect of them and vice versa – so agree it up front, avoid surprises.

- Everybody needs to feel some understanding, recognition and reward.

Your good people need a good environment in which to give of their best. A superb environment will not guarantee excellent performance, but it helps. Poor conditions, restrictive practices, and lack of support, will guarantee an uphill struggle to sap your strength.

4

Precursor to Performance Management

Are you ready? Do you know your environment?

Recruitment

Performance Management begins with recruitment – recruit the right people in the first place.

The luxury of recruiting from scratch the people you want working for you is not an option readily available to us most of the time.

You are more likely as a manager to have a ready-made team, fully established, warts and all, for you to deal with when you arrive in your new job either from another company or as the result of promotion or reorganisation.

However, the occasion will arise for you to recruit, and this is the only opportunity to get it as right as you possibly can. Recruiting the right person at least gives you a chance to gain the most out of the subsequent People Performance Management process and give your organisation the best possible results.

It just has to be worth spending the right time (whatever that is for the particular recruitment task) to be assured you have secured the best people currently available in the market place.

This book is not the place to document how to carry out recruitment activities, but there is one point that must be adopted in order to achieve success from the Performance Management process – you must be involved in the recruitment process, you must be involved at the interview stage and you must be part of the final decision-making process. That is common sense.

A word about ageism

Dangerous stuff! Very subjective, quite emotive, and difficult to handle. We believe it goes on! Recruiters seem to care less about it and are unlikely to admit it exists as judgement criteria within their selection process.

More mature employees, especially those out of work, hold a different view.

The subject is well documented – we all hear stories of prospective candidates having all the right qualifications and experience, being able to put a tick in all the requirements boxes, yet not even getting an interview. Worse still, receiving a letter actually stating that they have other candidates who better meet the requirements the employer is looking for!

Ageism is undoubtedly a minefield for all involved in the recruitment process and not one that can be addressed with much satisfaction.

Strangely, or perhaps not so strangely, ageism affects men more than women. It is often the case that an employer will seek to employ a more mature woman where the requirement is for stability, a solid contribution, experience in dealing with people, reliability in attendance and so on.

With men it is a fear of 'oldness' – a perceived inability to react and accept change, a slowness to grasp new techniques – concern that they are looking toward retirement, they are over-qualified, and are experienced in how to keep their job!

Alison Eadie once wrote in her Daily Telegraph column about the reality of ageism, countering the official facts that suggest the number of vacancies almost matched the number of people looking for them by suggesting the vacancy numbers have round holes whilst the job seekers are square pegs.

One of the big banks in the 70s retired early a raft of their experienced people with a view to reducing employment costs. Within a short period of time, the bank almost fell apart through a lack of experience throughout. Its fledgling employee base just did not know what to do within an industry which runs on experience.

Support from the business

One of the difficulties to be faced, certainly if you are a recent recruit yourself, is getting support from the business for the need to devote appropriate time to the recruitment process.

Often, HR swing powerfully into action with well-defined procedures designed to source the most appropriate candidates for you.

You need to be involved in the process and you need tactfully to be in a position of influence. After all, you, and not HR, have to manage the new recruit. You have that responsibility and you are accountable for any failings. HR will be seen as attributable to successful results from the new recruit during the first year!

Allow them their accolades in exchange for appropriate time to recruit who you want. Fight, fight, fight for as much time as it takes. Be prepared to dig in if the first round doesn't provide the person you have profiled. You don't get a second chance.

People involvement

No one likes being told what to do. It is another of those default human characteristics that seem so readily to cause a reaction.

'I'm new here and I see that you have been making sploggits for 35 years. Well as from tomorrow morning I want you to change the way you produce sploggits – no discussion, just do it'.

Sound familiar? Make you feel good? Comfortable with instant change?

The underlying problem with this is that you are being forcibly moved out of your comfort zone into the unknown. You have no say in the move and there has been no understanding of you and your environment and circumstance. You feel exposed, isolated, uninvolved and your are suspicious.

Oh and there is mention of the magic word 'change'.

Self-managers

A simple book is *The One-Minute Manager*. Okay, it could have been written in 16 pages instead of 96, but the principle is sound.

But how did *The One Minute Manager* arrive at that position? By the use of a Performance Management process that resulted in self-managed people working for him.

The process would have set out clearly, in simple terms, explicitly what was required of each team member. It would have required total understanding of the objectives and common agreement between employee and manager that each objective could be achieved – that all training and all equipment necessary to achieve success is or would be available appropriately. It would also provide an opportunity, a forum, to amend objectives or timings where external forces have changed the environment (the goal posts have been moved).

Self-managed people can get on with their tasks. They form a natural self-managed team because they all know what each other is doing – they have common goals and the incentive to succeed. Any drop-off in performance will be visible to the team and will be difficult to justify unless due to external forces or just having a bad hair day.

The team's manager is thus freed up to focus on strategy, in the knowledge that his team are actively on track with today's business.

Contracted hours

When analysing the operational complexity of the human being in the work environment, consideration should be given to the hours they put in.

The logic matrix of possible reasons for hours worked would probably yield greater permutations than the National Lottery.

Here, for example, are just some of the reasons why employees may work longer than contracted hours:

- a fear of redundancy
- hope of recognition that will improve any chances of promotion or pay increase
- a genuine liking for being at work
- a domestic issue they can't face
- a fear of failure
- a personal need to check and double check all that they do
- a lack of training in automation systems
- a stubborn resistance to accept time-saving systems in favour of labour-intensive ones
- a desire to get ahead of colleagues
- etc, etc

The ideal stance of course is to work the contracted hours and no more. That is why they are called contracted hours.

In reality, additional hours can arise from the employee's wishes or from 'pressure' from their employer.

The good people manager will be actively aware that the goal should be:

- for all people to work contracted hours
- to ensure when setting objective tasks that they can be achieved within contracted hours
- to ensure that work is completed within the contracted hours
- to provide training in time-management techniques where required
- to recognise the event when an employee puts in additional hours to complete an unscheduled task.

It cannot be correct to expect any individual to work beyond contractual hours on a regular basis unless that is a condition of his or her employment.

It must be the employees' choice to work additional hours, and to do so because they personally want to and not because they feel pressured by the business into doing so.

It is the manager's responsibility to ensure the well-being of employees who do work additional hours and to recognise the value of their contribution.

It is also the manager's responsibility to understand fully the reason for such additional hours. If there is a training or support need, it must be planned and scheduled, the goal always being for the employees to complete their work within contracted hours.

There are, of course, jobs where it is difficult to operate strictly within the bounds of contracted hours. If a customer 'demands' to speak with an account executive in customer service at 5:31pm about placing a £100,000 order, it will not yield the best results to tell the customer that you are going home now because you finish at 5:30pm and there is no one else here. Dealing with international customers also brings its own customer service requirements over time zones.

Most account executives who have a direct responsibility for a number of customer accounts tend to work hours which are outside their contracted hours, a decision they make themselves because they see it as a requirement of the job – they are better able to be successful in the job. By no means does that make it right, but they choose it as an operational requirement of such a job. Working these longer hours, owning the responsibility, should be, and usually is, rewarded by a higher level of remuneration.

I recall one such account executive who had a social domestic and pleasure reason for leaving at 5:00pm on the dot. He had responsibility for the biggest customer account in a business that operated 24 hours a day. The customer's senior director wanted information fed to him daily about his orders.

The director started his day early so the executive got to work even earlier and, without fail, checked the status of every order and the manufacturing plan for that day, and relayed this by telephone to the director as he was having his first cup of coffee. At 4:45pm the account executive sent a fax confirming all had gone well with today's plan, highlighted any order off plan and the corrective action being taken during the night, and then left on the dot of 5:00pm. This personal service approach worked well and the account executive managed to combine ownership of his job responsibility with his personal needs.

The environment

It should go without saying that personal environment is so important, yet this is an area that is often overlooked. We humans like our own set up, our personal preferences. It is important to us.

A significant difference in work effectiveness will be evident between employees who are plonked in a corner facing a wall with a walk way behind, and employees who are involved in where they sit, the direction they face, their immediate surroundings, the amount of sound proofing, seating, lighting, and heating. After all, we spend a large chunk of our lives at work!

Tools and equipment

Similarly a person will work much better and certainly happier when provided with the right tools and equipment to carry out the given tasks, even down to the provision of note pads, pens, post-it notes and so on. We work better with our choice of tools and equipment.

Summary of Opportunities

- Seize every recruitment opportunity, embrace it warmly, assign maximum personal effort.

- You must be involved in interview and selection.

- Strive for contracted-hour working.

- Provide the best possible work environment.

You have your people sorted, the environment is good, now you need a process.

5

A Performance Management Process

The guts of all you need

A definition

Let's be really clear right here and now <u>what is meant by performance</u> <u>management</u>.

 It is the process to manage employee performance by setting realistic objectives, tuned to business strategy and employee capability, that will be achieved or exceeded.

A script for each of the three players

The **employee**, the **manager** and the **business** each have important roles to play in the performance management process. These are serious responsibilities and must be planned in to the personal organisers along with appropriate time throughout the plan period.

Often, time for managing employee performance is allotted begrudgingly and under pressure. In fact that very lack of planning and acceptance of responsibility, creates subsequent pressure that should not have been there in the first place.

The role of the manager is to:

- recognise the strengths of each direct report
- set objectives and related measurable tasks for each direct report
- ensure each objective is in line with business requirements
- ensure each objective is relatable to the employee's job description
- ensure each measurable task is achievable
- ensure provision of equipment and training appropriate to assist the employee in achieving success
- request and review progress reports
- respond effectively to any off-target progress report
- keep a watching brief on, and take an active interest in, progress
- make notes of successes along the way, of employee style, use of competencies, and strengths, for use in the review
- work with the employee's colleagues to ensure a committed unit is focused on team achievement, removing obstacles as or before they get in the way
- offer advice and assistance wherever needed, appropriate or requested
- construct the clearest and easiest path for an employee to be successful in achieving the tasks that are set and agreed by both the employee and the manager as being achievable
- report progress to the business.

The role of the employee is to:

- understand and recognise his or her strengths
- participate fully in the setting of the performance plan objectives and their related measurable tasks
- agree to objectives/tasks only if they can be achieved
- plan and schedule each objective's measurable task and execute each plan
- report progress throughout the plan period
- report areas that are off-target, and their impact
- input to the performance review

- offer for consideration, where it is the case, development needs to expand strengths
- take an active part in the performance review to arrive at an agreed review document

The role of the business is to

- ensure there is a process in place for both manager and employee to embrace
- understand and support the process 100%
- take an active interest in the results that are achieved
- understand where the contribution has come from
- recognise where expectations have been exceeded
- value the process that has brought such contribution.

Avoid tabloid syndrome

Performance management is not an opportunity to bring down an aspiring employee.

Nor is it a process to rate individuals in a business-wide competition. We are all different, we cannot all succeed at everything in the same way. But we can contribute in areas in which we have competence and skill, with the right equipment and training, and with genuine support and encouragement from the whole team.

If the requirements of a performance plan have been met fully, in every way that was agreed at the setting of the plan, and yet the employee is deemed to have failed at the review, it is my firm belief that the business has failed the employee in some way (aside from illness or abnormal circumstance). How can it be the fault of the employee?

Also, part of the performance management process is a continual progress review through which any off-target performance is identified and highlighted before the end of the plan period. Thus the off-target performance is shared with the manager who then owns the task of determining a solution – the manager owns the responsibility because that is what people management is about. He may find the solution together with the employee, or with others within the business, but leaving it until the performance review and recording a failure on the part of the employee is not performance management. It is just plain dumb.

Performance Management – a way of life

The principles of simplicity and clarity of understanding can be applied to performance management to real effect when the organisation accepts the need for performance management to actively *cover its population in its entirety*, and to do so as a way of life.

It must not be seen as an us-and-them activity – a time to endure because the consultants persuaded the board that this appraisal system will generate improved performance from the people in the business.

It must be more than a paper exercise that comes up once a year, to be dreaded, feared, defended against. If it played out like this, then it will have little impact and will be seen as the process we have to go through once a year before we can get on with our real jobs – demotivating to employees and a waste of company time and money.

The traditional appraisal, that once-a-year activity that must be carried out, is feared and dreaded by manager and direct reports alike – it takes up time, it is confrontational, causes friction, generates bad feeling, strains relationships, and at worst the business can lose good people.

Yet if performance management is active as the prime focus of the manager all through the year, the review is just another part of the process and one that holds no surprises. If both employee and manager have been sharing awareness of performance, dealing with issues as they arise, they will be operating as a team. The review becomes a collection of the activities and achievements throughout the year.

By focusing on people, and the successful achievement of their objective tasks, throughout the year, you will promote the release of their skills and competencies and the full benefits that arise from them.

This is the opportunity to move away from tradition, to harness the catalyst to the biggest increase in the performance of the business – through increasing the performance of its people.

Performance management should link recruitment right through to the appraisal.

When you have an opportunity to recruit, you must devote appropriate time to the process in order to maximise the potential to be derived from subsequent stages of Performance Management.

It is the usual adage of put in the effort at the beginning, be really clear what you want and try to get it, and the benefits will be so much easier to realise.

Visible links

There must be a clear link between all documents relating to an employee role. Each document has its own purpose but the link should be clear.

The job description is the key document from which the others emanate. It develops upward to recruitment adverts and downwards into the performance plan.

The job description is not a working document. It is a plan, a layout of requirements – requirement of the *job to be done*, and indicating the *profile of the person to carry it out* – the appropriate attributes to be sought to best perform the role.

The flow should run as follows:

Job advertisement – a truncated version of the Job Description – should include the purpose of the job.

Job Description – this is not a working document. It is a plan, a layout of requirements for the job to be done. It should show the purpose of the job, show all responsibilities and accountabilities and give an indication of the profile of the person to carry out the role (skills and competencies, experience, education and so on).

The Job Description may relate or indicate a link to the Mission Statement.

Objectives for the current performance plan should emanate from the Job Description and relate to current business strategy.

Job Advert	Key responsibilities	Related to job description
	Key accountabilities	Related to job description
Job description	All responsibilities	Related to the job
	All accountabilities	Related to the job
Performance plan	Objectives	Related to job description
	Measurable tasks	Related to objectives

Recruiting

Where you have an opportunity to recruit, time must be well spent to attract the most appropriate candidate. The requirements of the job must be clear not just on the Job Description, but in the mind of the people manager.

I have seen some appalling job descriptions that are not only out of date but barely go beyond *'Please turn up between 9 and 5 every day.'* If you have nothing to go on from a bad job description, you will be inclined to make up the words of the recruitment advert which may themselves be out of sync with the business need. But if the job description is already completed, comprehensive and up-to-date, you simply have to lift the words. Make sure there is no reference to 'Must be able to work under pressure' though! You will not attract good, intelligent, experienced people with such words. Yet so often, these words appear.

'Join us and we guarantee to make you sweat, to give you a hard time every minute of the day. No relaxation for you to plan your workload, we crack the whip from 9 to 6 – and those are just the hours *we* work – *you* will work much longer than us!

If there is pressure, then this may be a reflection of poor management. If pressure does exist, then perhaps the recruitment advert should say: 'the main current short-term objective of the role is to determine how to remove the pressure!'

The recruitment advert for a job should, as most but not all do, demonstrate the key responsibilities and accountabilities with a clear distinction between the two.

This is an extremely difficult activity to carry out and get right. A lot of people managers either can't be bothered, just don't think they can do it, or plainly don't see the point. Similarly, if the process is not explained to individuals, they too will not see the point and just want to get on with their jobs or what they think their jobs are – and that is the whole point!

Equally, there is often pressure from the business to get the recruitment under way, get the person hired as soon as possible in order to relieve the pressure, and more than likely to dump a lot of the mess onto the new hiring.

Yet the benefit to be realised from this simple process is that if everyone is adhering to the tasks out of the current objectives, which are in sync with the job description, which has been written with accurate consideration for the genuine responsibilities and accountabilities of the role, the performance plans have a greater chance of being achieved as will the business goals.

Distinguish responsibility from accountability

The distinction between responsibilities and accountabilities may sound small, insignificant, and the need may even seem pointless. But in reality it is essential for an individual to understand what he is responsible for and what he is accountable for.

Responsibility is less active and has less effect. Someone assigned the responsibility to manage materials stock may be assigned accountability for obsolete stock at the end of the year. One is slightly more specific and with a barb of 'it's down to you mate'. But it should not detail specific levels or numbers. **Accountability** embraces both success and failure.

Another approach is to say that **responsibility** is being given the task to do and **accountability** is being charged with saying how well it was actually done (or not done).

Objectives

Objectives are the next level and are more specific. They are time bound and will therefore appear on the current performance plan to be reviewed for achievement at the performance review.

Objectives you set for your people to achieve must bear a relationship with the objectives set for you by your manager. The same is true for every level in the organisation, both upward and downward, so that you could gather all the objectives set for all the ground-floor level of people and they should add together to equal all their supervisors' objectives and so on to the very top – the company objective.

Some managers worry about determining objectives as if they must find new sets of words, new objectives and don't know where to look for inspiration. Look no further than your own objectives and it will reinforce the point that it is your people's success that makes you successful.

Objectives should be a combination of new and existing requirements. This is often misunderstood. Each Performance Plan is not an opportunity to rewrite a job description unless the job has changed.

It is therefore perfectly okay to have a regular, recurring objective year on year providing that is something the business requires. Just because it was achieved last year doesn't mean it is any less of a requirement to continue to achieve this year. After all, if nothing else has changed, why should it be any different?

For example, an objective may be set every year as 'Obsolete stock value to be no greater than 10% of all stock value at 31st March'.

In reality of course, some things will change from year to year or the business will die. Objectives may well remain the same in essence but some of the wording and numbers may change. Others will be replaced by new ones.

Whatever happens to objectives, the most important aspect remains the associated measurable tasks and these are far more likely to change each year.

Setting objectives is both easy and hard. Easy because the objectives you set must agree with the objectives that have been set for you by your manager, so you already have the data – there must be a link or else your group of people will be achieving the wrong goals.

You need to interpret the objectives set for you and translate them into objectives for your people.

The more difficult part is to determine the words of each objective that interprets your objectives as closely as possible, that are simple and clear to understand, and that can be measured for proof of success at progress reviews.

Measurable tasks

This is the most important part of the performance management process in terms of significance to, and relationship with, business results. Get success with these and the rest is a natural occurrence. Once agreed and set into the performance plan for the coming period, focus everything on the achievement of the each objective's measurable tasks.

Measurable tasks are the activities that are defined as necessary to carry out and complete in order to support achievement of the objective to which they relate. In proverbial terms, look after the tasks and the objectives will look after themselves.

Where an objective may set a requirement to control stock in Room 201, the measurable tasks will set out what actions are deemed necessary in order that the objective is achieved.

Treat objectives as a project and measurable tasks as the activities to be carried out, the project milestones to be achieved along the way. For example:

Objective 1

Determine and execute a disposal plan for obsolete stock in Room 201 by 31 March next year.

Measurable Tasks

- Carry out a full inventory of the stock in Room 201.
- The Inventory Report will include type of stock, value, date last used, on which process used.
- Determine with your manager the stock in Room 201 that can be disposed.
- Publish, to the Finance Manager, a proposed disposal plan and schedule.
- When authorised by the Finance Manager, execute the plan, reporting progress and results.

Now these are clear measurable tasks assigned to an individual and which also involve the manager. If all of the measurable tasks are completed, the objective must be achieved. However, there is a challenging requirement to ensure that the Finance Manager authorises the disposal plan within the schedule you set, but that is a task for you to manage.

A difficulty arises in determining how to assign a definitive figure. For example, in a Customer Support Centre, the objective could be set 'To improve call answering from 10 to 3 rings' which could result in failure if it improves from 10 but only to 4 rings! But if the objective is set 'Improve the call response to better than 10 rings' and the measurable task is set as 'strive to achieve a call response of 5 to 6 rings and no longer, through the deployment of xyz hunting technology', the objective is likely to be achieved (an improvement) and the team will find out what level of improvement was actually attainable and in the process will have determined what prevents them from attaining even better results.

It must be a success because it is an improvement over the previous 10 rings and also because if 7 or 8 rings is achieved, you have still been striving for 5 to 6.

Nobody has reason to feel demotivated because next year the team will continue to strive for 5 to 6 rings and maybe there will be an additional objective to determine and remove stumbling blocks that prevent 5 to 6 rings being achieved.

However, it is important that the manager accepts his objectives as being realistic to achieve, before translating them for his people.

Measuring the tasks!

It is important to note here how a task is measured as being successfully completed.

In the above example, there is a reliance on Finance to carry out an assumed action to review and agree the disposal plan. If Finance determine they are unhappy with the plan, or they consider the action a low priority, there is an opportunity for the tasks not to be completed in time and the objective will be seen as not being achieved.

As long as the individual has completed the elements of the task that can be completed, it is still deemed successful. The manager has a responsibility to assist in the element assigned to Finance.

After all, the Finance Manager is unlikely to be aware of this objective when it is set and may be heavily involved in other duties when the request for authorisation is submitted. The manager's support is required to communicate with the Finance Manager ahead of the request for review and authorisation.

At the review, it is not important to determine that the reviewee has been unsuccessful but what *has* been achieved, how it was done and what was attempted. The reviewee may have tried many times to stir Finance into action – that in itself is a recordable event. There is nothing wrong with recording that the objective was missed because of third-party inaction, as long as all efforts were made to try. The reviewee may well want to record that support was requested from the manager. If the manager failed to provide support then the objective would be difficult to achieve, yet the reviewee had done everything possible.

Similarly, under an objective to improve call-rate response to 3 rings, it is most important to determine when setting and agreeing the objective whether this is an intent – a direction in which to go – or a precise figure to achieve or better. It could be for example, that the current response time is 10 rings and the manager knows this is not acceptable but is unsure what level will have the desired, significant change to the customer satisfaction element of the business. The point of this objective is to gauge the benefit of an improvement on 10 rings.

The review should consider not only what figure was achieved, but how it was arrived at, what actions were taken, what efforts were made. Maybe 3 rings is a goal and something to strive for but is actually unrealistic. After striving, it may well be agreed that 4 rings is not only achievable (and an improvement over the previous 7 rings!) but the difference between 3 and 4 rings has little impact on the service provided.

The Mission Statement

Is this just another fad? Actually it is a necessary, common-sense tool to have. Applied correctly it is invaluable. However, of recent years, it has been mostly used as a marketing tool, a sales gimmick.

Sales and marketing people saw an opportunity to make money through additional sales generated by creating, publishing and promoting buzz-word mission statements that grabbed potential customers attention and made them feel comfortable to place their business.

There are some missions statements that are either bad, really bad, or the company should be sued for making false claims!

How often have you been waiting in the customer lounge of the local exhaust fitting company and read their two-foot high Mission Statement on the wall behind the customer service desk where the engineer is arguing with a customer about some work they have done badly? You have been waiting for 25 minutes and the mission statement boasts: *'We fit your new exhaust while you wait'* – exactly, can't argue that one, you certainly do have to wait. But their mission statement also states: *'At Bloggins & Snodgrass Exhausts, Customer Service Excellence is guaranteed!'* You then hear the man at the counter saying to a customer, 'I can't fit you in now, Madam, I have three guys off sick – don't you understand?' Who dreams these statements up and what happens to the link between them and reality, putting them into practice?

Let's face it, it is pure short-term commercial opportunism and comes back to bite the business, when customers get wise and that is long after the marketing boys have cashed their cheque.

Another popular mission statement is of the type: *'We aim to be the leading player in the Boxowidgets market'*.

Apply common sense to this one and what do you get?

- If there are 10 competitors in the market, they can't all be the leading player
- What is the measurement for leading player?
- Does it actually matter if your are the leading player?
- It is doubtful you will always remain the leading player – does that mean total failure?
- If you are the leading player by say, sales volume, does that necessarily mean your business is successful, or that your service is better than the lowest sales-volume player?

The mission statement should be exactly that – a statement of the mission the business is currently on, a one-line strategy message letting the people in the business know what it is trying to do.

Apollo 13's Mission (initially at least) was to land a man on the moon. The objectives would have been something to do with bringing soil samples back, trying out some new kit, and testing astronaut moon-walking duration and so on. The mission statement for the NASA moon mission team would probably have said, *'To land a man on the moon and get the team back safely'*.

Mission statements are often misunderstood by the people in the business because the concept and purpose is not fully understood –

there is poor communication emanating from a lack of confidence in what it is all about. I have seen all-embracing mission statements going on for two or three pages.

There seems to be a mistaken belief that the more wordy the mission statement, the more bullet points it contains, the more meaning that can be crammed into it, the more buzz-words of the day it contains, the more effective and noteworthy it will be.

The common sense view must be the complete opposite.

People will fail to understand the message because they can't see it clearly, the statement will not be remembered in its entirety, the requirements will not be carried out fully, it will not reflect reality.

What are we here for?

A diversion of thought – what are we here for?

A business exists to make money, never mind what its mission statement says. The business is there to make money.

'We strive to satisfy every customer need' is a fine statement and a good reminder/prompt for all employees of the business, and it is certainly common sense. The business would not last long if its mission statement said, *'We strive to really upset every customer at every opportunity'* or *'We just don't care'*.

But a mission statement is a tool, not a result. The result we are looking for is to make money. If you want to argue this point, please put this book down and pick up *'The Beano'* because you clearly have not understood the first principle of business – the business exists to make money.

Positive benefit from the mission statement

Mission statements have their place and I would argue that it is not for external view. Common sense will tell you that if you carry out the words of your internally-confined mission statement, the results will be visible externally. They are self-selling, you don't need to shout about them. Externally lauded mission statements usually mask a lack of confidence in the business and may lead to complacency.

A mission statement should be simple, clear, readily understood, and meaningful. It should ideally be no longer than one sentence.

The best mission statement you can have (unless money is not a requirement) is: *'We are here to make money'*! Why do you need anything else? Even your customers can't argue against it because in the first place that is what they are there for, and secondly, they don't actually want you going out of business, despite their demands for you to reduce the cost of your supply to them. They need to be assured that you are financially healthy.

If your statement says: *'We are here to provide excellent service at the best possible prices to our valued customers'* and you promote it through marketing and sales, you are inviting your customers to challenge it with: 'Well, I think your service is less good than I expect and I pay a too-high price for it.' What options does that give you?

No, you are better off making use of a mission statement internally, and not using it as a marketing/sales tool.

A nice, simple, short and to the point mission statement will focus the mind of everyone who reads it. It will link in to job descriptions and objectives.

'We are here to make money through cost awareness and service that meets market demand'.

With this one, the CEO, MD, functional manager, machine operative, admin assistant, can all ask questions of themselves as well as of the business, such as:

- Are we making money?
- Are we wasting money? Am I wasting money and could I reduce it?
- Am I cost aware? What does it mean and what can I do?
- Have I saved money today?
- Have we improved a process and reduced cost?
- Do we offer customers what they want?
- Are we developing new services or products in line with

customer feedback?
- ... and so on

It is debatable if you should interpret the company mission statement into local ones for each department. It can be effective because it focuses the department on the part it is playing, but it can also be confusing.

If your mission statement is like the generic one above rather than a specific one, then there is no need to create local ones.

Who determines the words?

My personal belief is that if the top operational person in the company cannot write the mission statement on his or her own, taking note of whoever they are accountable to (chairman, board of directors, group, shareholders et al), then they are not worthy to hold office.

To me, that is common sense. Yet how many times do we see a person holding that very office embark on a survey, a competition, a brainstorming session, to arrive at a consensus. Surely to goodness, if the top man on our plot is unable to tell us in a short set of words what we are here for, then we are in serious trouble!

Amending the mission statement

This book is not intended to offer advice on whether a Mission Statement remains set in stone or is amended every year. It is very much a matter of what is appropriate for each business.

Changing it every year, however, does suggest a lack of confidence and stability, and perhaps the mission statement is even masquerading as an objective.

It is also a matter of satisfying the needs of the current environment. For example, a decade or so ago I recall a Mission Statement that said: *'To deliver our products and service in a timely manner, to meet our customer quality expectations, cost effectively.'*

At that time, delivering on time was paramount and a competitive argument. Focusing on quality was also significant, and costs, well, that one was in there for the supplier to be cost aware.

Today, all three – Time, Quality and Cost – are default expectations. They have been overtaken by changing demands of customers. If you are unable to deliver within 24 hours from receiving an internet order, or your quality is not consistently above 99.9%, then you are not in business for long, if at all.

As for cost, well it comes right at the front for the Supplier because of the current environment's demand that prices will be ever less expensive. A programme of continual removal of cost from the supply chain is the big issue today.

Quality and timeliness are more quietly controlled by specific processes developed over the last decade that make the need to emphasise these attributes less significant.

So, the need to amend or not to amend the Mission Statement must be debated and a result agreed.

If it is not, then the business is indicating that it doesn't care about, let alone understand, the importance and significance of the Mission Statement. In effect, it is saying that it does not understand its own business, the environment in which it operates, or the market it serves.

Debating the appropriateness of the current Mission Statement as an annual or other time-period agenda item indicates that the business does understand itself, the environment in which it operates, and the market it serves.

The Mission Statement for Apollo 13 was amended and quickly too, the minute the effect the failure of two of the three life support modules dawned on the guys at the Houston Control Centre. 'Houston, we have a problem' led to an amended Mission Statement along the lines of 'Get these guys home' with objective number one being 'alive and unharmed'. Landing a man on the moon became instant history for this mission.

Interestingly, what the team then did was to conduct a performance management plan process in days rather than a year. They concocted measurable tasks to support the objective and then measured the results. If they didn't achieve the expected result, they came up with new ones until they got it right. They set the tasks in concrete and prayed. The tasks were successfully achieved and so the objective was achieved. OK, there was a big chunk of luck in there somewhere too.

Further examples to clarify the point

If a business determines that its mission statement shall be: *'To double sales over the next two years'*, then clearly the statement should remain effective for the duration of that period (unless, of course, something goes dramatically wrong with the plan).

Should it say: *'To develop a new technology within five years'*, it might want to determine a new mission statement if the new technology takes significantly more or less time to develop.

Further, a statement may say: *'To provide the service of Widget Clonks to Snoggs, Bloggs, and Cloggs in line with their technical requirements'*, which means the statement remains valid even if the technical requirements change. But if Snoggs, Bloggs, and Cloggs disappear from the customer list, and are replaced by Toogs, Poogs and Noogs, maybe the statement should just refer to 'our customers'.

Preparation for the Performance Review

The personal organiser alarm beeps to give notice to the employees and to their managers of the impending Performance Review.

This is the *full-term* performance review. Many performance management systems propose optional reviews during the full review period.

Personally, I believe that if the full review is annual, then progress reviews should be carried out at least at 6-month intervals but preferably every quarter. Monthly reports and project reports will provide progress information but are no substitute for a one-hour, one-to-one review. Performance reviews are about more than the work being done. Interim reviews can be informal – if the manager and the reviewee so desire. After all, performance management requires honesty, openness and trust and this is sometimes difficult to attain if there are some awkward items to discuss and both manager and reviewee know that the meeting will be documented and filed with HR. Performance reviews don't just deal with the nice things. Addressing difficult issues is part of the process and the manager and reviewee are best placed to determine how a successful outcome can be achieved. The full-term review is different – it is a formal process.

Interim reviews should be fairly brief, controlled by the manager but without pressure to complete them in a defined time if there are still important issues to resolve.

There is little to be gained and a lot to lose in finding out at the end of the year that things went pear-shaped seven months ago and the objective has not been achieved. Seven months ago is when that should have been recorded and a solution found through the use of an appropriate solution seeking tool (see Part 3 for use of EALs).

The effective people manager will have been reviewing performance throughout the review period and will have built up document notes on progress against the plan. The manager will have encouraged the reviewee to do the same.

Thus the more efficient and effective, the more cordial and easy each review (interim and full-term) is to carry out.

It becomes an almost rubber stamp exercise to document what has gone on through the review period which means the principle of simplicity and clarity of understanding are being utilised.

Who is reviewing whom?

One of the most useful tools in support of a performance review is the 360 degree review.

The reviewee chooses colleagues, peers, and others with whom he or she has working contact, to provide a few paragraphs describing the reviewee as seen from sideways-looking eyes. This less formal review can, and should, be made none-too-structured so that it is genuine feedback about the individual and can be interpreted in support of actual performance.

Some books suggest only peers should carry out 360 degree reviews, others say, in the case of a manager being reviewed, their peers and their direct reports. I maintain that anyone who the reviewee chooses, who knows the reviewee in work mode should be invited to provide feedback. However, it is most important to ensure that anyone invited to provide a 360 degree review understands the requirements.

There is often an understandable reticence about 360 degree reviews. Oh, my, they will say something awful about me or they are my best friend so it will be good news, or the opposite.

In my experience I have never found any 360 degree review to be anything but a reasonably accurate reflection of the way it is as seen from the reviewer's eyes.

It is actually quite difficult to write a completely false review of somebody. Firstly, your name is on it and your own credibility will be brought into question.

Secondly, in order for it not to be challenged, it should be backed up by evidence. This applies to good and to less than good reviews. If someone walks on water, we would like to know the date and time the event took place!

This is why it is so important to ensure a 360 degree reviewer understands what is required. As usual, it is a sprinkling of common sense, simplicity and clarity of understanding. 'Mary regularly demonstrates good leadership qualities, like the time she made the decision to do x y z in the heat of a customer complaint, and set the standard for the way we all do it now.'

360 degree reviews are gaining favour because people are seeing their value as part of a performance management process. However, 360s are more usually offered as a voluntary tool. They are not always mandatory and the number of people selected is up to the reviewee.

It may be that reviewers have difficulty not only in interpreting 360s but in knowing what to do with them, where they fit in to the performance review. An objective achieved is an objective achieved, and a strong 360 comment such as 'Mary's contribution in dealing with the crisis in March is a typical example of her leadership competence' may be easier to include in the performance review than 'Mary is a joy to have around the office – she is always there when needed'.

360s continue to hold some degree of fear and apprehension. This is understandable because it takes the performance review perceptibly outside the confidential zone. Other people are included in the personal, one-to-one review. Others have an opportunity to influence the review of performance.

Then there is the issue of who sees the 360s – the reviewer? The reviewee? Both? Should those selected to give feedback share that feedback? This is an important point and a clear policy is needed. There must be consistency in its application and adherence.

Those selected for feedback must also understand the significance of their role. They must allocate time to give proper consideration to their feedback – it is just as serious and important as the review itself.

There may well be a major training requirement to provide awareness of the significance and value of the 360 degree review.

The Performance Review

Formally recording results is a simple exercise in the performance review word-processing document. The measurable tasks were set at the planning stage and documented under each objective. It is a simple matter of opening additional space in the word-processing application to record results against each measurable task.

Objective 6.

Ensure the continuity of performance in the in the event of absence, planned and unplanned, of Service Team 2 personnel.

Measurable tasks

- Determine activities required to be covered

Review: This was achieved, a list exists, the manager was involved where appropriate.

- Develop the process appropriate for execution

Review: The process was developed with involvement and input from Service Team 2 personnel. Three meetings were held which you chaired.

- Seek and obtain agreement from proposed resources

Review: Following some heated meetings, which threatened to stop the development, you took a leading role in doing x y and z

- Document the process and publish its location

Review: Document exists and is stored on the server with hard copy in the Quality System Library. A copy is archived off-site.

Don't forget that the task can be part achieved, carried forward, and still be classified as successful if there is supporting evidence to justify preventing its planned completion. It will depend on the circumstances but remember this is not a time to persecute your people. You need them to successfully achieve their objectives.

All this simplicity of recording provides time to focus on other performance issues, to talk about how good or bad the year felt, and to plan for the next review period.

Because the Performance Management process is on-going through the year, the review evidence builds up so that reviewee and reviewer will be aware of levels of success in achieving objectives before the full-term review takes place.

However, the full-term review is not a mechanical process. Well actually it is, but it needs the additional application of skills and competencies to weave a careful path through the element of emotion.

You cannot document a mechanical process for dealing with human emotion. We humans are affected by so many influences, we can be quite unpredictable. We will often say what we don't mean and not say what we do mean. As employees in business, we are not trained psychiatrists. We can only do our best making the fullest use of the tools available.

Every manager of people should certainly have acquired knowledge of such tools (and gained experience of them during role play exercises) on an intensive training course such as Positive Power and Influence, or similar.

Time allotted to the review should be appropriate to ensure the employee feels his or her performance has been thoroughly examined, discussed, understood, and recorded accurately.

Too often, managers block book performance reviews into all the mornings of one week and conduct them at the same pace, with little concern at all for the emotional pace of the individual whose performance is being reviewed.

This does not mean that the reviewee dictates the pace of the review. It is a joint effort here between reviewer and reviewee to ensure that the review is fair, honest and effective and will require all those same skills and competencies gained on a Positive Power and Influence course.

For example, the use of 'moving away' can be very effective when stuck on a review issue. 'Let's take a break and come back to this' will often result in both parties seeing the issue differently when resuming and able to reach an unexpected conclusion.

This book is not the place to look for detail about the mechanics of a review – how to record the results, or document training requirements and development needs. Each performance management process will be different and each company will have a different culture and philosophy and policy.

However, whatever is agreed as necessary on-going actions resulting from the review must be planned, scheduled, published and actioned accordingly. The action list tool (see chapter 6) is an ideal and very effective tool to use for just this kind of activity.

Performance ratings

To rate or not to rate? If you do, just how do you rate employee performance?

The reason for the questions is twofold.

Firstly what is the purpose? Why is there an obsession to rate employee performance?

After all, we are recruited because we are seen to have the skills and competencies required. We are given a job to do, objectives to achieve, tasks to complete in a given time.

If all is done to satisfaction then the rating is clear – 'OK', 'Job done', 'Mission accomplished'!

Records of the achievements are maintained, a career library is built.

So why rate performance and introduce all the human emotive and differential qualities unnecessarily?

Was Neil Armstrong rated on his performance when first setting foot on the moon?

Well, Neil, I am sorry to tell you that you only get a 'B-' for the moon landing. You see, your speech was impromptu and didn't score too well in the 360 degree reviews we got back. Your voice wasn't too clear and you hesitated in the middle. But the main failing was forgetting our sponsor – you were supposed to have said 'This is one small step for man and one giant leap for mankind – this Mission is brought to you by The Wally Shoe Company – they always leave a big impression wherever you go.'

Secondly, what is a suitable rating scale?

I have actively witnessed reviews which rate performances:

- 1 to 5
- 1 to 10
- A B C
- A B C D E
- Excellent, Good, Poor
- Outgrown job; Exceeds requirements of job; Meets requirements of job; Meets minimum requirements of job; Developing in role

There must be others.

More worrying than the rating scale is the variance in its

application. The rating scale will be applied with each manager's interpretation and this should bring cries of 'unfair!' although of course a reviewee will not be able to compare assessments.

Some of the issues with rating performance are subjectivity, human emotion, inconsistency in reviewer viewpoint, and locally interpreted application. Even following intensive training in the performance management process, there will be variances in the application of the rating scale between reviewers.

You only have to look at the environment of football referees. These guys are professional, trained, qualified, regularly assessed, and carry out a job that makes most supporters wonder why they bother! Yet they all do it differently. Their Assessors will mark their performance for each game providing yet another opportunity for interpretation and variance.

Most rating systems have an associated script which defines the meaning for each rating mark. Whilst this guide is useful if not fundamental in matching performance evidence to the script to arrive at a rating, the process is still subject to interpretation and to personal bias.

The script can also make it easy to qualify a reviewer's rating decision.

Let's have a quick look at some of the popular rating systems

1 to 5

Everybody gets a 3. Well they do don't they? Okay, a new starter may get a 1 if that is reserved for such developing people, and there will be the odd 4 where somebody is ripe for promotion or movement within a grade. But mostly it will be 3s that are awarded.

The script will probably say 'competent performance'. A 2 will reflect badly on the manager. Everybody can't be promoted, so there will be few 4s and the script for a 5 is reserved for water into wine converters. So why bother with rating? If you must use 1 to 5, don'! Use 1 to 6 – it has no mid-point – you must justify a 3 or a 4.

Oh, and why not ask your manager as he sets your objectives, 'What do I have to do to get a 5?'

1 to 10

With such a wide choice, it is easy and a normal human characteristic to go for a range within the range that has its own meaning. For example, a range of 4 to 8 where most people will get a 6 or 7, the best will be granted 8 and those in need of development will be given 4 or 5 almost as a point of emphasis or segregation. The biggest difficulty for the manager is in designating one reviewee a 6 and another a 7.

Then there is the situation where one reviewing manager uses the range 6 to 10 and another uses 4 to 8. This will be closely followed by some pretty disgruntled employees.

It is bound to cause on-going concern and bitterness and may take months of effort to remotivate the people.

Again, what is the point?

A B C

There is little room for differentiation here. If the local policy is 'Nobody gets a 'A' rating unless they can turn water into wine', then everybody gets a 'B' or a 'C' which results in 'What's the point', or serious demotivation for anybody receiving a 'C' they don't agree with, especially if they are the only one and feel their performance it little removed from that of their colleagues.

Oh, and what is the point of having 'A' if it can't be applied?

In a desperate attempt to make up for the inadequacies in rating range, I have seen managers expand the range by adding an unofficial '+' and '-' so the range extends from 'A+' to 'C-'. I have also seen 'A/B', 'B/C', 'C/D' used. Again it introduces inconsistency between reviewing managers and the message reviewees receive is confusion, unfairness and lack of positive commitment on the part of the reviewer.

What is the point of this rating system at all? It serves no purpose.

A B C D E

An improvement on ABC in that it provides more scope. But that 'E'! Wow! It shouts at you that it is there for one purpose and one purpose only. No manager is going to give any of his direct reports an 'E' unless he would rather they found another job. It screams 'Bad performer, I don't like you and I never will'.

Excellent, Good, Poor
Nuff said!

Outgrown job, etc
This is one of the better rating systems. It provides information supportive to the review of performance in two ways.

Firstly, it suggests that if people perform in line with what is expected of them they will allocated **'Meets requirements of job'**. This is not a mundane performance but a good, competent performance from a valued contributor

The policy must set out clearly that this is the rating designated to employees who have done the job they are employed to do, who have met all their objectives fully.

This company is comfortable in the knowledge that if most employees receive this rating the business is doing well in maintaining its direction.

Secondly, employees feel comfortable to receive 'Meets requirements of the job' because they are aware of its meaning and recognise that there is less emphasis on ratings and more on what has actually been achieved in the job.

To compare this system with the 1 to 10 scenario, any of the higher ratings are achievable but difficult to attain in other than exceptional circumstances and backed by demonstrable and qualifying evidence. **'Exceeds requirements'** is designated to an employee who has met all requirements with the addition of one or two added contributions which have enhanced the business by adding value above expectations. There must, of course, be justified evidence to support the rating and it should be a significant additional contribution to warrant the mark.

'Outgrown job' means exactly that – this is a signal to the reviewer's manager that this employee is ready to be considered for promotion appropriate for his/her skills and competencies.

The interesting point here is that the rating need not necessarily mean that all objectives have been met and exceeded beyond wildest dreams. It is an indication of consideration for promotion – the employee is ready for greater or changed responsibility, a new challenge, or new environment. It could even be conceivable that the employee has just met the requirements of the job, but because the manager is tuned in to what is making the reviewee tick he has determined stagnation is setting in – the employee has much to offer but can do no more in the current environment.

At the other end of the ratings scale, **'Meets minimum requirements'** is designated to an employee who clearly has some difficulty if reaching the performance expected and is a signal that some TLC and attention is required from the manager to work together to raise the performance. What it does not suggest is that this is a poor performance – this company tries to recognise that it employs good people.

'Developing role' is applied to a new hire or an employee recently promoted into a new role with insufficient time and evidence for an effective and fair review.

Other rating issues

In some systems, if not the majority, a rating is required not as an overall assessment of the performance but for each objective that was set and for behavioural characteristics too.

All this does is to exaggerate the perception the reviewee already has, make it more difficult for the reviewer by having more to rate objectively and to introduce further subjectivity into the review and thereby water down the significance of the performance.

Worse is to come! Having rated each objective and each behavioural characteristic, the reviewer is then asked to give an overall rating for objectives, one for use of skills, one for use of competencies. Oh, and by this time the review becomes less of a review of performance and contribution, and more a personal one of the reviewee!

How does the reviewer arrive at an overall rating when using the

ABCDE system? If there are 10 objectives and all score 'B' except one which has a 'C', what is the overall? What if three have 'C' or 'D'? Who cares? The reviewee, that's who. Does it add anything to the process? Does it detract from the value of the process?

Gone are the days of loyalty of service. Today is all about self investment. In some industries, the average length of service with a company is around 2 years.

Thus an employee could conceivably receive only one full performance review in their time with the company.

So, what happens to the performance review and its attached ratings?

Well, the company maintains records in the event that ... er ... um ... well, they maintain records. The employee may just return at some point in time and then their old records with their performance ratings can be ... er ... um ... no! ... I don't think they will, because firstly it is from a different time zone, secondly a number of record maintainers and reviewers may have moved on by then and the prodigal son may not even be remembered.

From the exiting employee's viewpoint, ratings are insignificant and to a potential new employer they are relatively meaningless. Of far more significance and importance is a set of words that summarises past performance. Not the rating, because any recruiter knows that ratings are subjective and assigned by the manager at that time and in that environment. What was actually achieved and how it was done is what is important to the recruiter.

When you attend a recruitment interview, you will be asked by the professional recruiter what you actually did, what achievements, what difference you made, how you went about it, what value you added. You will not be asked what rating you achieved in your performance review!

Ratings reprise

I am sure there are industries, and indeed companies, that make good and effective use of rating performance. That is good and if everybody is happy with it, fine.

For me personally, I consider rating performance:

- a cop out of people management – a failure of really knowing your people

- a mechanical requirement set by consultants who introduced a performance management system constructed in Academialand

- moves the focus away from the performance, the contribution, what has been achieved and how, in what environment and circumstances

- demotivates those being reviewed

- can lead to inconsistency

- serves no useful purpose other than to provide a role for HR filers to carry out, which in itself serves no useful purpose!

Matters arising from the performance review

Many things will occur within the confines of a performance review. There should be no hard and fast rules on how the review should be conducted – just a framework, a set of guidelines, within which to operate.

The manager has overall responsibility for the review and for ensuring that any actions arising are documented, and actioned through the use of a management tool such as the Efficiency Action List described in Part 3.

Such actions might be to provide equipment, training or reorganised environment, appropriate to ensure successful completion of a measurable task by a certain time. Employing the use of an EAL will dig deeper into the requirements, range of available equipment, costs, impact of the measurable task and so on.

Any significant impact to the ability to complete the task as originally agreed should be documented so that this is clearly taken into account at the next review.

Summary of Opportunities

- The reviewer, reviewee, and the business itself each has a role to play in the performance management process.

- Performance management is recognising, encouraging the use of and developing strengths. It is not about putting people down, identifying perceived 'weakness'.

- There must be a link of words and meaning from recruitment through to the performance review.

- Make performance management the way of life – not a last-minute activity once a year.

- Accountability has a different emphasis to responsibility.

- Objectives need to be realistic and be supported by measurable tasks, and be linked to business objectives.

- A mission statement is an essential tool when applied correctly.

- 360 degree feedback is valuable supportive evidence.

- Rating performance is a questionable exercise.

Part 3

It's All You Need! –
The Other Essential Bits

You need proof that the process is working. Is your ship on course?

If you are unable to determine where you are and where you should be, you are equally unable to make course-correcting decisions.

You may as well crash on the rocks and be sure about it … if only you knew where they were!

6

Audit, Report, Review, Action!

You need to be assured that the process is working in accordance with the plan. You may need to take action.

You need information; a health check on the business. But how much information and what type – and what do you not want?

Check the health of the business

Having implemented your performance management process, your people are busily and enthusiastically working away on their objective tasks. They, of course, need no day-to-day close supervision, so there is nothing for you to do until their scheduled performance reviews.

Er ... well there is actually, because you need to know the effect of their efforts to confirm the accuracy of the current plan.

Everything they do, every enhancement they make is impacting the business in real time, and you need to be assured that everything is going to plan whilst you turn your attention to planning future strategy. It is equally true of what they are not doing. Time lost may be difficult, if not impossible, to regain before the end of the year.

You have a dual role to perform and to juggle it with the other important aspect of your job, planning future direction with your boss and the rest of the company at whatever level you are required so to do.

Your roles are both tactical and strategic:

● **Tactical** through support to your people (a) when they request it and (b) when you can see where you could help maintain the direction

- **Tactical and strategic** as health monitor – how is your part of the business doing? What is going on? What needs attention? Where is action needed? Is the business on course? Is future strategy impacted?

- **Strategic** as you develop your part of the plan for the future – this may be a direct set of objectives from your manager, or your own pursuit of cost savings, improved throughput, enhanced customer response, improved information and visibility and so on.

Support to your people will be mostly as and when the need arises, in response to issues highlighted in progress reports, and at times of periodic performance reviews.

Health monitoring requires information to analyse, which means you need to determine what it is that you need to know. The information must be presented in simple form for clarity of understanding, it must be provided quickly on demand, be accurate, and as automated as possible.

So what sort of information do you need and only need, and how can you receive it simply and ensure clarity of understanding?

Results information service

Without receiving information, you are driving blind. Make a turn and it could be the right decision, the wrong one, or completely unnecessary.

You need information that tells you where you are, in which direction you are going, at what pace, when you will get to your destination, and whether you are on or off course.

Before you receive information, you need to determine what the information is that you actually need, precisely what information, and only that information.

We are bombarded by information every minute of the day and even then we probably receive only a tiny amount of the information that is available.

Yet a very high proportion of the information we receive is neither needed by us nor relevant to our main job responsibilities. This superfluous information saturates our minds which requires unnecessary time to search for the information we really do need. Our overall effectiveness is reduced because we are not focused on relevant data and take longer to take corrective action.

Unfortunately, we humans are a nosey lot. We enjoy gossip. We like a good story. So if data comes our way, we are most likely to have a look at it rather than dismiss it out of hand as irrelevant.

Strong personal discipline is required to focus the receptors on relevant and meaningful data from which to build awareness knowledge and make decisions.

You must avoid the clutter, filter out the information not required, and focus on the material that is specific and significant to you at this point in time.

You may choose to delegate the task of compiling and presenting data, but take care to ensure this is already set as a Measurable Task or you may invoke Clause 99!

So what information do you need in order for you to make decisions that maintain direction?

You need three types of information reports.

- Monthly reports
- System reports
- Problem-solving/solution-seeking reports

Monthly reports

The first information you need is to be assured that the Objectives and their associated Measurable Tasks that you set for your people are progressing to plan and schedule.

Monthly reports provide you with progress status for the objectives on which your people are working, and highlight any unexpected issues that may impact the Plan.

This feedback is traditionally provided in the form of Monthly Reports from your people, perhaps with the addition of specific progress reports if appropriate.

System reports

Next you need to know how the business within your area of influence is performing as a result of your people's progress on their objectives. This information should be available from within the business system. It should be available either as raw data for you to interpret and turn into the information you need, or as finished information reports that the business has designed and determined as being what you need.

You may want to ask the System Administrator to develop information reports to suit your specific needs.

System reports provide you with business performance data – outputs, downtimes, customer calls, service records, sales figures, stock records and values, actual against budget, financial data, a health check on the pulse of the business

Problem/solution reports

Now, what about the nasties that come up unexpectedly? How are you going to know about them, control them and ensure they are completely dealt with in a formal manner?

Problem/solution reports provide you with assurance that those unexpected issues and concerns that arise courtesy of the Laws according to Mr Murphy and Mr Sod, are being managed through to conclusion that limits their impact on the overall plan so that direction is maintained.

This last piece of the information jigsaw is how to deal with issues that lead to progress slow-down, project slippage, extended completion schedule, of which you will be aware through visibility of the above two information sources.

You need an effective tool to deliver an optimum solution in these circumstances and preferably one that incorporates the need for common sense, simplicity, and clarity of understanding.

There is little else you need.

Let's look at the three information tools in more detail.

Monthly reports

Yet another paradox!

A strange phenomenon in business, to which managers are subjected, is the division of business time into neat little chunks. Managers condition themselves to work to these time chunks and plan to make use of their skills and competencies only when actually in the closing stages of a time chunk.

As an example, the business operates from year to year and this is probably the biggest time chunk in the business calendar.

Yet all managers become extremely industrious toward the end of this big time chunk, affectionately known as 'Year End'. They become far less active and focused during 'Month 1' – the next size of actively adopted time chunk below the more financially functional 'Quarter' or 'Q'.

Yet the business is a continuum. One day follows the next. A problem is still there tomorrow unless dealt with today. The year doesn't actually end.

The paradox is that it would appear more natural for the human being to work in a less well-planned way, to react to the time chunks on the business calendar rather than to determine what information may be needed at any time and plan for it to always be available on demand.

One of the most discomforting situations in business is when the Chief Executive asks for information at a time earlier than that decreed on the calendar, and at very short notice. (Mr Murphy will of course have a hand in the re-timing of the event that normally takes you 6 hours, but rest assured that Mr Sod will be there to ensure that notice of the change will be served no earlier than one minute to five!)

But this simply will not do if we are employing common sense, with simplicity (which of course we are). We need the system to work for us not against us.

Let the system work for you

Remember that the business is a continuum. It is live and buzzing all the time. It does not stop at 5:00pm and restart at 9:00am the following day. Only humans do that.

All sorts of fun and games can be generated by Messrs Murphy and Sod from a midnight flash flood, through early-hours burglary or vandalism, to a burnt out main circuit board only available from the Californian supplier on 5-day ship time (see Contingency Plans in Part 4). Your best-laid plans are there to be messed up.

When it comes to writing the dreaded monthly report, it always seems to be left to the last minute and is generally carried out in a frenzy of searching through the diary to see what has happened since last month, and looking for things that sound impressive.

Drafting the monthly report as you go is so much easier and less stressful than trying to write the finished article at the last minute where you can bet your mortgage that Mr Murphy will fill that time with unplanned, unexpected delights to soak up your valuable time and create untold pressure.

Note that for the purposes of explanation we set our frequency chunk as monthly because that is the most common type.

It is strange how many styles of monthly reports exist within an organisation. Each produces its own style and content.

You may not be successful with any attempt to try to convert everyone in the company to your style so I doubt it is worth the effort. What is important, however, is that you have a style that suits you, that is simple, clear, easy to complete, to archive and retrieve and that you manage to persuade your direct reports that this is the style to use.

Just let them see the benefits, the simplicity, what you want and what you don't want, and that's it – they'll go with it.

Don't write your monthly report!

As a manager of people you don't need to write your own report. Far better to make use of simplicity. Get your people to write it for you. Make use of their monthly reports and the cut and paste facility in your word-processing software.

There is nothing wrong with this. As long as the information is true and accurate, why reinvent the wheel? You are not employed to rewrite words. Your role is to ensure information flows up the chain simply and clearly, with you acting as filter to absorb data relevant to you and enhance, endorse, emphasise information you want your boss and peers to have sight of. Simple and quick provision of clear relevant business information.

If you try to write your own report from scratch and your boss does the same, there is a danger that the message from the bottom changes its flavour by the time it reaches the top.

Take the following as an example:

'My supplier is giving us serious problems but I am working with them.'
'There is an issue with a supplier but otherwise okay.'
'Supplier issues are being addressed.'
'No issues with suppliers – we have a process to address them.'

You will have things to say about what has been achieved this month and what you are planning to do next month. What you are planning to do will form the basis of what you actually do next month. This means your next Monthly Report is already written as long as the plan is achieved – you just need to change the tense from future to past!

You will also need to report issues of a nature that may have serious impact on the business and certainly those outside your area of influence, responsibility or authority.

Your monthly report should be no more than one side of A4, and only 3 headings are required:

- Achieved this Month
- Planned for next month
- Issues and concerns

Ideally under 'Achieved this month' will be progress reported on objectives. Other things may well have been achieved but they should be one-off, occasional items, or at least related to your objectives, or else you are off-course, dealing with somebody else's objectives at the expense of progressing yours.

119

Items in 'Issues and concerns' may well find themselves the subject of an Efficiency Action List (see EAL later in this chapter)

You may need to educate and train your people in this method and style of reporting in order to keep the whole thing simple for yourself.

If you receive reports from your people the day before you are required to submit yours to your manager, and your people have followed your style, you have a simple cut and paste job – only the relevant and significant bits – followed by some careful editing as required to maintain the maximum of one side of A4. The tough bit here is to condense the reports from all your people into one report for your boss of no more than one side of A4. But that requirement focuses the mind on the really significant issues.

So, part of the education of your people will involve imparting the message that one side of A4 is a maximum and if there is only one sentence of relevance and significance then that is fine. It does not make their report look any less important or make their contribution during the period seem any less great. It is not about waffle, it is about communicating information on progress status in the name of awareness, and inducing action where required. Four pages of waffle with no substance, impresses no one.

As an example, a developer working on a sole software product should only report that the project he is working on is on or off track. If it is on track, and there is nothing known that is likely to impede progress at this point in time, then there is little point in reporting anything more.

Incorporating common sense and simplicity here, there is little better than listing out the major objectives set for the year and reporting progress on each. After all, they are mostly what your job requirement is for this period. The bonus in the simplicity department is that at the end of the year you have 12 records of progress with any issues and concerns that arose. A straight cut and paste into the Performance Review document.

By listing all your objectives on your monthly report you are prompted each month to determine progress on each and report it. There may be some objectives that cannot start yet but you may still want to document it on your monthly report to maintain awareness (and before your boss asks you).

It is debatable whether monthly reports should highlight forthcoming holidays because the super-effective manager should already be aware of that, but we are only human and a reminder can save a little embarrassment. Holidays, to some degree, are irrelevant to the requirements of the monthly report because holidays should be built in to the development plan at the outset and there is thus no additional impact on the plan.

Be careful how you deal with a requirement to report output data or service statistics, or other business data requested by readers of your monthly report.

If the requested data is regularly requested, and it is short (i.e. able to fit in the Achievements This Month section without pushing the whole report over the one-page-of-A4 abyss, then make provision for it as a template in your standard monthly report so that you just have to fill in the figures.

If, however, there is a lot of data and it requires a presentation emphasis, then do not put it in the Monthly Report. Treat it as a separate exclusive report, either attached to the Monthly Report or distributed independently. Better still, if a shared network is available, put it there and reference where it can be found.

Maintain records

It should go without saying that the most effective way to complete a monthly report on your computer is to save last month's report with this month's title and overwrite the body of the report with this month's new and exciting stuff.

Keep it all in a folder titled MonRep and you have 12 records of achievement at the end of the year from which to edit your year summary should you be so requested to do. Always good stuff for updating the CV.

System information

It is not possible, nor would it be correct, to advocate precise system data to look for in your specific business. There is no model format, no generic layout. The data available will be specific and the requirements will be unique to you and your business.

However, what is important here is how you go about getting at the data and what you do with it.

You have an opportunity to let your mind loose, to attack the data with wild abandon, and to be constructively creative with what is reported.

Your mind will be looking for those crucial data that provide the significant indicators to the real health of the business.

There are two types of system information available to you – that which you can see and that which you can't – well, not readily at first, anyway.

Most managers settle for the first type because it involves less work, the system provides it already laid out in presentation form which is recognised and accepted by the rest of the organisation, and it is not subject to criticism or question – its integrity is sound.

This is the stuff built into the system when it was installed. The system will readily churn out vast data reports reflecting everything that has been input.

Because these are recognised as *The System Reports,* they will be more readily accepted, if not expected, across the organisation. There is probably a standard requirement for managers to report this type of data periodically. Whether anybody actually does anything with it is another matter. At least it keeps some poor administrator employed collecting the reported data, combining it, formatting it and reissuing it to managers in the form of a company report of results that each manager files in the appropriate ring binder on the shelf that holds ring binders.

The other type of information is the stuff you can get yourself by:

- poking around the system within your area of authority
- by asking others with higher levels of authority to provide certain pieces of the jigsaw (this information will probably require social refreshment in exchange)
- making use of your mind's flair. Set it loose as a hitchhike around the system asking the galaxian question 'Why?' Add a

few 'What ifs' and the odd 'How much' and you will be rewarded with a treasure of information previously just lurking, unseen.

The performance manager will go in search of this information in the certain but blind knowledge that he will get some advantage. He knows from experience that he will find something that will add value to the decision-making process.

This is what performance management is about. Not settling for the norm. Doing that little bit extra. Testing to see what might happen. Asking the question. Pushing the envelope, as they say over the pond.

Anyone can report output of 300 sploggits with an efficiency of 96% but do they know why? Do they know what the circumstances were? Do they understand what prevented the achievement of 97% efficiency? Are they actively analysing the data to see how 320 sploggits can be achieved or 300 with no rejects? It could be that 50% extra effort and cost would be required to produce 320 sploggits. But removing a previously unseen obstacle might generate another 5 sploggits for next to nothing.

Some years ago, a guy reporting to me said, 'I just don't understand why you spend so much of your time looking into the system. Now you want me to report this new stuff you think adds value. It will take me an extra two hours a month. I don't see the value. What's the point? Who is it for?'

Even when everyone else did see the value, he remained sceptical. It is no bad thing to have a sceptic in your team – it ensures the actions you take are challenged for you to justify. You need that. It ensures as much data as possible are validated and most importantly that they are validated within the team and not by one individual. The team shares the validation and therefore owns a chunk of its success.

This customer service guy remained sceptical because his mind was fixed on the extra two hours work he was required to put in per month. His mind was so focused on the additional workload that he just couldn't see the value. Yet what the data actually told us was that one of our customers wasn't worth dealing with on the current prices scale. The customer, an awkward case to manage and requiring significantly more time than others in the portfolio, would not negotiate a new price scale at a time when a new customer was secured at good prices, by the sales team.

Guess whose customer the time-consuming, low-price one was? With this customer gone to soak up our competitors time, the customer service guy found a saving of much more that the additional two hours originally required to produce the data.

The two hours of course soon became minutes because this type of search for available but previously unseen data spawns a continuance into automation – get the system to do it for you.

I am not suggesting the removal of every customer who is not currently profitable or whose orders require abnormal time to manage. There are other solutions and today's problem customer may be tomorrow's salvation. It was the right decision in this case.

The point is that the business was unaware of the problem and therefore was not looking for a solution. Yet the information was there all along. Nobody had looked for it. Nobody asked 'Why?'

The performance manager will not wait for the business to react a month later to his submission of required routine data. He will be looking for the meaningful stuff and making course adjustments in accordance with results of analysis. He knows his plan, his input to the budget, will not be perfect. That is why it is a plan, a budget – something to aim at from the best input knowledge available at the time. So he doesn't wait for somebody else to make a course correction decision whilst hiding behind the budget which is no longer accurate. A budget becomes inaccurate the minute it is issued. The world changes. There are many external influences.

The performance manager is active, reactive, searching the horizon for clues, indicators. If he can't see the horizon for the fog, he will seek alternative information. He should encourage his people to follow his example and thereby maximise results.

Information review meetings

There should always be a meeting, or meetings, scheduled to review information reporting the health of the business. These are important meetings as they are the one opportunity to fashion the shape of the business for the future.

Therefore meeting time is opportunity time and needs to be used wisely. The meeting is not an opportunity to present data and to impress. It is about interpretation – determining what the data is saying in line with expectations, and about action – agreeing on course correction where appropriate.

I have attended meetings where managers present their data to the meeting in the same way it has already been circulated and reported. Thus the manager soaks up valuable meeting time presenting what is already known. The performance manager, obliged to report data in the corporate manner will present to the meeting only active solutions to any problems he has identified within his data. He will not go through every detail of the reported data that the audience already knows – unless asked to do so from the point of clarification. There is just no need.

Obvious stuff, I am sure you will agree, but how often have you sat through a 'one-hour' meeting that is into its third hour because some manager is droning on defending his poor performance? Or the entire meeting debates some data of poor performance as a group remote from the department that has performed poorly.

Where performance is off track and you have to take corrective action, where some data you have found tells you bad news, or where problems arise at any time, you need the assistance of a tool – one that is common sense, simple to use and leaves everyone with a clear understanding of what is happening.

Efficiency Action List (EAL)

Call the process what you will – I chose Efficiency Action List for no other reason than it is a list of actions necessary to take in order to maintain or raise efficiency. Simple common sense, clear and understandable.

I develop a list, on my computer, of issues for which solutions are actively sought, as an index or summary sheet. It shows a meaningful title, date the issue was raised, current progress date (i.e. date of last meeting).

I then create a separate file for each issue with headings as follows (which mimic the EAL process too):

EAL process

- The issue *(a simple and easily recognisable title for the issue)*
- Circumstances in which the issue arose
- Impact *(a statement of potential negative and financial impact the issue is giving the business)*
- Solution *(this is the progress section which will show the results of progress meetings to determine an eventual solution – this section will expand until the solution is found)*
- Benefits *(financial benefits of solution implementation)* and any downside
- Approval requirements prior to solution implementation
- Implementation plan and schedule, for the solution
- Implementation progress record against plan
- Audit *(measure effectiveness, check negative impact is eliminated, reduced or contained, check benefits are being received)*
- Archive *(maintain completed EAL in the library of solutions)*

EAL (Efficiency Action List) is a good tool to use when faced with the need for a solution to a problem.

It is a common-sense tool adopting the principles of simplicity and clarity of understanding.

It is not a highfalutin, all embracing, complex tool requiring a 5-day off-site course to learn the basics. It simply addresses the requirements.

Efficiency Action Lists are exactly that – lists of actions which if implemented will yield efficiencies. A simple approach to deal with any size of problem and can be used by anyone at any time.

Other problem-solving techniques can be adopted as appropriate within the EAL process. The basis of EALs is to control the process that turns a problem into a solution by recording the problem and its impact in order to be able to see what needs to be done to remove it. The key is the constant recording of everything that happens and when the next action is planned.

How it works – the EAL process

Keep all such problem/solutions in this electronic document (the EAL) so that a record is maintained of all solutions achieved. Everybody will be reminded of success, there is a record to refer to if the same problem arises, and people know what has been achieved during the year.

The computer folder named EAL (or whatever you want to call it) should contain one catalogue file and a separate file for each item added.

The catalogue file is no more than a list of items addressed and should comprise a unique reference number, a simple short title, the date raised and the date completed (or 'on-going if it is still being dealt with) for each item.

It needs no form of category or severity rating to signify importance because what is important to one person may not be important to another and the EAL process tries to treat all issues the same.

Each item file should start with a definition of the problem, a record of the circumstances, the environment in which the issue came about.

The reason for this is to maintain a historical record so that it can be referenced:

- whilst a solution is being sought, to maintain focus on the original problem and to test the solution
- at any time after a solution has been implemented so that if a similar instance occurs, this one can be compared
- by people who may have an interest but who are not directly involved with the issue. You may need their support and they may have some input.

By recording an explanation of the circumstance surrounding the appearance of the problem, it also saves time in subsequent solution-seeking meetings and avoids interpretations and false judgements being made.

The circumstances should comprise a couple of paragraphs maximum. This is for tidiness and not for space saving – if more is needed for clarity or because of complexity, then use it.

Next, record the impact the problem has had, may have, or will potentially have on the business. This may be in terms of:

- additional or unbudgeted cost
- lost productivity
- missed schedules
- missed opportunities
- extended completion times
- unexpected quality issues
- external/third party failure
- any consequence resulting from the problem

Remember that whatever the tangible source of the problem it will have a cost. There is always a cost and the only thing that really matters is the cost.

Therefore, next add the benefit(s) of finding a solution – which should be a mirror image of the impact and cost of the problem. It is important to do this because money savings focus the mind better than anything else and seem to grab the attention of senior management, especially those in the finance department.

Determine people appropriate and relevant to seeking a solution.

Then document the plan – how the solution might be arrived at.

There may be an initial brainstorming meeting (document who was there and the main points – if there are many, refer to a separate meeting report – and the date of any follow-up meeting and who will attend).

Publish this to relevant personnel – all of them, because, even if not directly involved, they may have some invaluable input at some time and if they don't want the document they will soon tell you.

Adopt the same principle with subsequent meetings, always publishing the full history so that everyone can see what has gone on, where it came from, and whether you have been here before and so on.

The solution will form part of an on-line library of solutions which make up the EAL, for people to browse around and print off as they wish. It shouldn't be necessary to circulate it – it should be made available to all.

One benefit of adopting a simple system such as the EAL is that it can be used to seek solutions for anything that has a significant negative impact on the business. It was used once where an administrator was regularly working 15 hour days in a significantly important job and was clearly stressed out. Although most of the job functions were routine, it also involved customer contact adding unpredictability to the stress.

There appeared to be nothing in the performance plan that required such consistently long hours to be worked in order to complete the objectives. The problem screamed time management as the solution, and in most cases the employee would be despatched on the next available course – problem solved.

The problem was added to the EAL because the next time management course was two months away. A team was raised to look at all potential solutions for the hours worked, including whether the performance plan was overloaded.

One of the first and obvious solutions to arise was to book the employee on the next available time management course! The course was booked and the employee attended and gained much from it which was subsequently employed to good effect.

In the meantime the team broke down the elements of the job and looked at how it was carried out; it soon became clear that significant chunks of time could be saved by focusing on the important and urgent tasks and pushing the other tasks down the priority list.

The significance of the EAL was that it could be seen as a less formal tool than some consultant-installed, company-supported, costly process, with tons of training. It was seen as an almost personal tool to try to solve a colleague's personal and serious problem.

The employee felt good because the problem was highlighted which demonstrated that people understood there was a genuine problem and that they cared.

As it happened, the workload was not seen as overburdening, and time management played a big part in reducing the hours. But the EAL process identified work practices that would otherwise not have been found. The employee was carrying out some tasks that were not even required, and spending vast time on other tasks because they seemed to be important. A quick go at the game of 'leave it and see what happens – the ones that come back and bite you are the ones that are important' soon removed a big chunk of work.

Importantly, there was not one but many solutions found. Other people were able to make use of them too.

Summary of Opportunities

- Make sure you know what is going on.

- Be aware of achievements – put a tick in the box on the year planner.

- Be aware of off-plan/slippage issues – be prepared to raise these issues and give support to get back on track.

- Otherwise leave your people to get on with their jobs – check the system reports for the effect.

- Only receive relevant progress and system information - discard the rubbish, it will soak up your time with no reward.

- However, do search the system for data, filter it for the good stuff, see what it is telling you – there is some good stuff in there.

- Monthly reports are important but keep them short, simple, clear – don't rewrite them as they move up the chain; filter and edit.

- Develop your own simple tool to manage issues through to solution implementation – a combination of solution seeking and project management.

Part 4

Life Is Not Predictable

If only life could be that bowl of cherries! But then we would win the lottery and performance management wouldn't matter any more. Oh how boring life would be then.
Thank goodness it isn't like that!

7

Difficulties and Dangers

How to get it really right or completely wrong!

No half measures

If no formal performance management process exists, the first and biggest difficulty you will encounter is acceptance from the organisation to fully implement a performance management process to which everyone is utterly committed, and that is genuinely a mainstream control across the company and at low cost.

So here we meet yet another paradox. The company prefer to buy in to the latest fad costing hundreds of thousands of pounds because they feel they can justify it on two counts.

1. Everyone else is doing it (the Sunday supplement says we must have it or we will fall behind and the consultants have sold us on the benefits).

2. There is a psychological boost to those within the top management team that they have justified their exalted position somehow by authorising the go ahead, and will be perceived as making a good decision for the business.

Yet the company tends to shy away from fully supporting the less expensive, more simple process that is already there and available for immediate use – the process that should be a default within every good people manager; the ability to clearly communicate what they want from their team members based on an understanding of their capabilities and their job description; the application of common sense, simplicity and clarity of understanding.

This leads to the third reason top management is more inclined to support the expensive third-party, off-the-shelf system. They are reluctant to own the process because people management is an uncomfortable area to step into. It is far easier to sign a huge cheque and sit back to watch a consultant waffle and train, train and waffle, leave and then expect it all to work perfectly. If it doesn't do what the consultant said it would, then it must be the fault of the middle managers.

It will be equally difficult to achieve full success if a performance management process, and the available information systems, are already active in your organisation because (unless both are working fine and achieving the results expected):

- it will be an uphill struggle to take it all back to the beginning and introduce commitment from everyone to improve the results

- it will be seen as a failure, an admission of defeat, which will affect the degree of confidence in the top team proposing the improvement action

- it may require some organisational changes (deliberately political or necessary) in order to justify the decision and gain the confidence required.

But you must persist. Failure to sway opinion will come back and bite *you*, not the others. Your job as a people manager will be all the more difficult because you will have less of a process within which to work and because you will be expected to get consistently good results from a system that scoffs at the need to understand people. There will be a question mark over you if you don't get results.

People managers

There will always be difficulties with the management of people just because we are human and not (not yet anyway) clones.

No two managers are the same, which is why this is one of the most difficult aspects of people management and indeed of process management too. Difficult for two reasons:

Firstly because any failure on the part of the manager can be covered up by using a whole range of reasons and excuses.

Secondly, yet of equal if not more importance, a direct report can feel unfairly treated, can see the differences between manager styles and results, and can feel helpless. If they appeal they are seen as complainers – HR may be informed, involved even, entries may be made on files.

'It doesn't happen,' I hear you say. Ha! Who are you kidding?

Very few managers are good people managers. Very few people are naturally good at people management.

They may be technical experts in their field, they may know the process inside out, they may know their markets better than anyone else, and they may be well respected and get on with everyone, yet still fail to recognise the power or see the potential in the team they are assigned to manage.

Managers tend to focus on the manufacturing or service process and on the pressing objective of the time rather than on the people that can achieve that objective.

This is yet another paradox because it brings us right back to involvement, inclusion, the basic needs of human beings. Back to the differing motivational circumstances that affect the way we work. Yet the manager (himself or herself a human being who can be touched by the same feelings) ignores the blindingly obvious.

What about pressure on the manager who would really love to apply performance management? He may have pressure from his boss to do this and do that, 'Never mind what you think you are here for, just do what I say and do it now!' He may also have pressure from his people too.

You can do it locally

Fortunately, you can employ your own performance management system almost unseen if one doesn't exist and the company won't buy your sales pitch.

You may have to accept the job descriptions if they are owned by HR, but there is usually an opportunity for you to input to them and to recruitment advertisements as they arise.

You can take the objectives your manager sets for you in the company system and from there on it is your field of play.

You interpret your objectives for those you set your people and their related measurable tasks. Nobody in the organisation other than your own people will either see or question how you manage your people providing the results are re-interpreted into the company system following reviews.

You should have no difficulty in getting buy-in from your people once they see all the benefits of simplicity and clarity of understanding – and that they get a big chunk of the benefits because you are more focused on them and their success. They will understand your message that you are only successful if they are successful, something that is usually missed by direct reports – they assume you are on some other mission unrelated to the objectives you set them.

I have known direct reports seriously believe their manager is there to spy on them or to close the department down, or at the very least to reduce head count. Unfortunately, there will be occasions when one of these is a reality, but mostly there will be very few managers working to some clandestine agenda.

Make sure you do your job!

Another encounter of the difficult kind is to maintain your personal activities to the requirements of your job.

This requires use of techniques acquired from a course on Positive Power and Influencing skills and techniques.

The classic manager trap is to accept tasks assigned by your manager throughout the course of the year without considering the impact on your performance as a people manager. There is a natural assumption, and perhaps an obvious one because of visibility, that you as the good people manager have time on your hands because your people are clear about their responsibilities and are busily attacking their objectives.

Well, if you are doing it right, this is exactly what should be happening, except that the time you have generated is for your other two areas of responsibility:

- health monitor
- helping to develop strategy.

The difficulty for you is to be able to challenge the tasks your manager is assigning you. You need to distinguish between tasks that fit into either Health Monitoring or Strategy Development and those that are outside of these responsibilities and are actually additional workload that your manager is dumping on you.

Difficult indeed! But you must develop a method for dealing with this. Failure to do so will undoubtedly result in watering down your effectiveness as a people manager and it is you that will feel the impact later on. A sort of double wammy.

Clause 99

Help is on hand however.

You need to invoke Clause 99. Once your manager has witnessed it, he will become wary of dumping because he has seen the colour of the Clause 99 card and knows it is within easy reach in your back pocket.

Clause 99 is that little get-out that managers always add to your job description, objectives, and anywhere else they can sneak it in to their advantage.

It is usually right at the end and says something like 'To carry out any other tasks as and when assigned by the manager'. Great! In other words do anything I tell you whenever I demand it, even if it is not in your job description.

Clause 99 gets its name from the '99' ice cream upon which you can heap all manner of toppings. The more you add the better you feel, especially when adding hundreds and thousands! However, an hour later you start to feel sick and wish you hadn't eaten it because you realise you took on too much – more than you could handle.

Now, you need to turn all of this to your advantage and in order to do so you must go along with Clause 99, but you must influence the wording. Again you will use all those skills acquired on that Positive Power and Influencing course to get your way here. Nothing else will do. You must win. You must be prepared to fight this one – you stand to lose the war, not just the battle, if you don't.

The words need to say something like 'To carry out other tasks related to the job, as and when assigned. However, should the level of tasks so assigned impact the ability to successfully complete tasks already assigned above then this performance plan shall be the subject of review and amendment, if determined appropriate'.

If your manager finds difficulty in seeing this blindingly fair statement and fails to accept its inclusion after application of your techniques of persuasion, assertion – and vast cups of moving-away-style coffee – then you need to look for another job or be prepared to be dumped on from a great height.

Similarly, of course, you must include Clause 99 in each performance plan for your people. By offering it as a matter of course your people should be impressed by your fairness. You must, of course, mean it.

Knowing me, knowing you

A mirror image of a people manager's performance is the performance of the people he or she is responsible for managing.

In other words you are a reflection of your people. You can only be as successful as the level and quality of objectives they achieve that are in accordance with those set. That is why they are your most important asset. You want them all to be successful.

With or without a deep knowledge and psychological understanding of your people, there is always the risk of unpredictability. There are so many potential opportunities for Mr Sod and Mr Murphy to work on with people and with their environment. The interactions and combined might of these two killjoys can have a devastating effect.

Thus, if you know your people well, have access to good reliable progress reports and information, have contingency plans in place and regularly reviewed, you have at least an opportunity for your best shot. But you cannot afford to be complacent.

Buzzwords

There are so many buzzwords forced upon the world of business today, it's a wonder we survive the pressure of the continual hype.

The danger is that the hype is powerful and self-creating.

It would seem to be that if you don't keep up, you will be left behind. You must at the very least be aware of the latest terminology.

The difficulty is in avoiding the hype, especially if someone influential in you company gets hooked.

Here are just some examples of buzzwords whose impact has affected us over recent times.

Culture change
'In order for us to implement the actions necessary to remain competitive, there must be a change of culture'.

How many times have we heard that none-too-old chestnut?

What on earth does it mean? What is the speaker of those words actually trying to say? More importantly, does that speaker actually understand the words and their intended meaning?

The reality is that culture change is a management cop out. It is an excuse for the fact that it is not working as well as expected, that we are facing severe competition, we haven't got much idea what to do, but we know it needs to be different. Therefore we need to change something, and it must be to do with the employees. Like there are too many of them, they are too expensive, the products cost too much to make, our lead times are too long, our customer service just isn't customer service, we are no longer at the forefront (our competitors do it better).

If only performance management health monitoring linked to distributed strategy development had been in place with full involvement, recognition and ownership across the people structure. It is then less likely that the words would be formed on the speaker's lips.

Nissan doesn't need a culture change – it changes itself every day – through the employees' continual quest for improvement everywhere.

The old adage that Japanese companies had no fear in showing Europeans round their plants remains valid today – 'By the time you catch us up we will have moved again and remain beyond your reach'.

Empowerment

Here is another of the regulars in the buzzword box. As if it is something new, revolutionary, that unless you have attended a 5-day course and survived, you will not be empowered and will not be able to empower others. It is so technical and advanced in its application that you will not understand it. Bolony! It is another piece of common sense wrapped up in consultancy megahype. It has always been there and available to you.

All it is saying is let the guys and gals doing the jobs have a say in how it is done today and how it is developed for tomorrow. Oh, and before we start, could you let us have a look at the mission statement so that we are all pulling in the right direction.

It was radical when first introduced, undoubtedly, but still common sense. In fact it was lacking common sense not to promote it.

Misused though, it can be very dangerous. For a less effective people manager, it can be a tool for escapism. 'I have empowered my people, so it is their fault if it goes wrong' or 'My people are empowered so I don't have to do anything anymore'. Worse still, the company may use it along the lines of 'Your people are empowered now so we don't need you anymore!'

More likely though is 'We operate empowerment here which means that, er ... um ... well ...can somebody help me on this one?'

Emotional intelligence

This is a buzz label for one of the newest kids on the block in the world of management fads. Emotional intelligence also provides the classic example of how to make money through the application of inadequacy blackmail.

Talk it up, breed the hype, publish lots of eloquent books by well-respected authors who impress with their 500-plus pages of techno-babble. Reviews appear in newspapers which make us feel totally inadequate because we don't have the slightest idea about the subject, and at today's board meeting the chairman nailed your coffin down when he said, 'I read a very interesting article on emotional intelligence at the weekend – I would like to know what our plans are in that direction. In our position in the market, it is clear that we should have full implementation as soon as possible'.

Well, as it happens, emotional intelligence is particularly relevant to *Performance Management – It's All You Need*. But not because the hype says 'I told you so'.

I just do not believe that there are many people managers who have read from cover to cover a book on emotional intelligence, but it looks good on the desktop next to the PC.

Emotional intelligence – the reality

For those of you who are still awake, and for those of you who are very awake because they have that board meeting to attend next week where the top item on the agenda is 'Emotional Intelligence – your role in our implementation plan', let me reassure you that EM fits comfortably and happily under the umbrella of common sense, simplicity, and clarity of understanding.

It is, in fact, desperately fundamental to performance management because it requires us to see others as they see themselves and as they see us, their environment, and everyone else around them.

It emphasises the need for accepting performance management as *the* process and not a sub-process. As a people manager, the requirement is to understand the people reporting to you so well that you know where they will perform excellently, you know what they will do, how they will react, and you care about that because you are able to use that knowledge to positive advantage for you, for your direct reports, and therefore for the business.

An analogy might be the astronauts on the ill-fated Apollo 13 mission to the moon.

I just don't see how a film, a Hollywood blockbuster, would possibly have been made had it not been for the total understanding each of the main players (the astronauts in space, the technocrats and administrators at Mission Control, and the back-up astronaut in the Simulator) had of each other's strengths, abilities, and likely reactions.

Without that emotional intelligence the astronauts would have died through CO_2 poisoning or burnt up on re-entry.

Sure there was a lot of luck riding with the guys, but EM played a really big part. Yet not once did I see a reference to emotional intelligence, the boffins rushing to the library to read up on it so as to predict likely scenarios. It happened through normal, natural common sense.

Why are authors of books on such subjects as emotional intelligence unable to write their missives in 128 pages? Just to give us a flavour, a quick understanding.

That way we might give it more consideration and if we understood it better, we might just buy-in to it and put some committed, enthusiastic and genuine effort into promoting it throughout our business.

Lean manufacturing

As against what?

If a manufacturing business employs a process of fat manufacturing (unless you are in the animal food processing industry) it will not remain in business, let alone be competitive, for very long.

Thus being cost effective within the operation of your business has to be a given – a default modus operandi. You will be focusing on Just-In-Time supply of materials and parts, you will have planned the implementation of automation where possible, you will have a plan for continued automation, flexible labour skills will be in place with a continuing training programme and so on. So why the buzzword? It is common sense.

Hands-on

The recruitment advertisement says the company requires a hands-on director. What in the name of good business operations does that mean?

Is it akin to management-by-walking-around – that gem of the 1980s? Are you required to push buttons on machines, or to carry out quality checks twice a day?

If it means you need to keep in touch with your people and what is going on in the business, well that is a major part of any job as a manager of the business, surely. The last thing we want is a hands-off manager isn't it? Surely you don't have any of those do you?

Work under pressure

'You must be able to work under pressure', says the job ad. Oh, that is really motivating. What this is trying to say is that if you join us you will be lucky to see your wife and family much before 10:30 every night (you will have left them at 5:00am) and you will be on call over the weekend and your telephone number will be distributed to everyone in the business so that they can contact you and only you to ask what to do in any emergency no matter how trivial. Oh, and if you need to contact the boss, you can't but you can leave a message at the golf club.

'Oh and just one more thing – when you join this outfit, we want you to have fun.'

These words are a cop out for the senior management in the business who have got the company in such a mess they are unable to find the way out and it has become the way it is. But they don't want the problem, so they employ someone to aim all the flak at.

We don't want you to help us find a way of relieving the pressure – we have no plans for that – we just want you to be the pressure sponge.

What incompetent management! A total lack of common sense.

World Class

How so? How measured? Somalia is in the world. Perhaps it is not considered an industrial nation.

What is the alternative? Could there be classifications like village class, town class, county class? Could there be a league table with promotion and relegation?

What is the difference between world class and a global player?

No, this is all about the need to appear different. The ad men and marketing boys and girls have been put to work to provide leverage in the competitive arena. So that we appear to operate differently (only better of course) than our competitors, in a different environment, and to be involved in doing something special.

Appalling recruitment wording

I read an advertisement trying to recruit people to join a very well-known national company in which it was described as 'having brands like X, Y, and Z'. It not only *does* have those specific brands, not *like* them, but it also *only* has those brands – it has no others!

It went on, 'All your determination and drive will be needed to …'. What else would you do with your determination and drive, use only some of it?

Another read of 'truly global sourcing'. I have no problem with the global sourcing bit, but 'truly'? As against 'pretending' perhaps? Or does it mean sourcing every square inch of the planet? 'Hoskins has spent two years sourcing the upper reaches of the Amazon and reports that he could find no potential suppliers of tooth paste tubes.'

'Global sourcing' to me indicates a freedom to source anywhere in the world where a benefit in supply may be achieved. Truly global sourcing must be ...er ... um ... answers on a postcard please, enclosing six packet tops from any Kelloggs product. Kelloggs, a truly global company!

Recruitment

However, should you be in the position to recruit, it is worth looking at some right and less right ways of going about it. There is no absolute model. However, spend time, be involved, be clear what you want and don't want. Don't let HR tell you what you want or who you should have. It must be your decision. Use HR. They are your tool to do the donkey work for you and allow you the freedom to think clearly and use your judgement.

Be prepared to fight for the right (and cost) to have a second go if the first campaign fails to deliver the person you want. Better still, get HR to write the rules for the agency so that, should they not produce acceptable candidates, you don't pay – okay, you at least get a discount for a second go. The agency should work for their money.

Should you have to accept second best, know what you are in for and make that clear to your boss and to HR. Document it. Time is a great excuse for memory loss when things go pear-shaped. Avoid the blame culture later – have the discussion now as a team – agree the potential consequences together.

Also, take an eyes-wide-open approach. You could be in for a surprise. The new recruit could turn out to be your best team member when given the opportunity, some time, understanding of their modus operandi, and your full support. Maybe they will bring something to the party that could work if you changed your style – you could learn from them.

There is also the danger of accepting that all spoken forth from the interviewee's mouth or the achievements enscribed on their CV is bone fide.

You will have your own style and tool box of interviewing skills on which to call, but do challenge, and be brave enough to challenge again if something smells off-course. After all, the interviewee is in sales mode. He or she wants you to buy and they already know that you are in the market. They know what you are looking for and they know what you won't want to hear or find out about.

They are certainly not going to offer their failings readily.

A danger some recruiters find themselves facing is where the most suitable candidate requests a favour. They will only do it when they are confident of a job offer (i.e. you have led them to this conclusion). At that point, which can be your weakest if you are desperate or have undergone a long and arduous campaign, they throw in their demand.

They catch you off guard. You are not expecting it. The danger is that you may commit verbally to something you could regret later – something that could set a precedent and cause ripples through the organisation and come back to haunt you. Your judgement could come into question.

Therefore have your response ready for such occasions. Expect it.

This is a great opportunity for a Positive Power & Influencing tool, 'Moving Away' such as 'I'll get back to you on that' or 'I'll need to consult with HR and let you know their view'.

Recruitment is a luxury

You usually inherit people. If you are new to the business, have been promoted or have moved as a result of reorganisation, the team in front of you is the one you have to work with, warts and all.

So you have to be a player in the game of acceptance. You can win the battles – you must win the battles – but it may be some time before you win the war and therefore you may maintain only your position as general, answerable for both success and failure. But then that is the job. Your team reads acceptance as tolerance. They will tolerate you and your new-fangled approach to managing them according to the usual rules of human existence.

Let them see that you will allow them to carry on as before and you will achieve a high degree of 'tolerance'. Change the whole plot on day one and you go to war. Strangely, the outgoing manager appears to have walked on water and done no wrong. That usually means he was happy for them to remain in their comfort zones, un-stretched.

Your initial performance plan will undoubtedly be more difficult than subsequent ones – you have some proving to do and they will want to test and challenge you because they will be all too aware that you may just be about to move them out of their comfort zone.

Be aware too that the quicker you change things and the more things you change, the stronger you will need to be and the more alone you may become. Your changes will have to bear early fruit too.

Recruitment reprise

If you have the opportunity, and there is no better one, put all the energy you can muster, use all the skills at your disposal, to get the right person. Even then things can go wrong, but at least you will be safe in the knowledge that you have tried and could not have done more.

There will be the occasion when despite all your best efforts the new recruit still performs outside your expectations, and you do have the responsibility to deal with that, and you must, difficult though it will be.

Nothing in life is perfect or predictable.

I recall an American who, many years ago, recited a phrase to me, the origin of which I know not, 'Every so often life will throw you a curve'. I remember at the time thinking how strange is the American version of the English language, but the meaning is there and it remains relevant.

Inheritance – tough decisions

If you inherit managers, supervisors, team leaders, reporting to you, it is imperative (if you are going to be successful) that these are the right people for you. They may be good people, but are they inappropriate for you? It may be tough but you need to determine if you need different people – and take action quickly. Your success and performance can only be a reflection of their capabilities. You are limited by that. If you need to make change decisions, do it tactfully, of course, but do it!

Psyche? Who's a psycho?!

Psychometric tests are used more and more frequently at times of recruitment and business reorganisation.

These tests, of which there are several well-recognised types, must be used for what they are – an indicator. A very good indicator too, especially if carried out in an appropriate environment, by qualified people trained and well-versed in the process, and with a good understanding of the emotional state of the person being assessed.

I have witnessed an individual psychometric test being carried out on seven people en bloc seated round a rectangular table in a small room. One speedster finished in a ridiculously quick time, cleared her throat, tutted and sighed, and stared intimidatingly at any of the others who looked up.

I have seen tests carried out on people at times of significant personal or work stress with inevitable results.

Whilst the tests are usually implemented by a trained person (who has the necessary one-off-use documents) I have been tested by unqualified egotists who have acquired the documents, or the software, and gone on to proclaim amazingly unexpected and spectacularly revealing results from their untrained interpretation.

Appropriately qualified and professional assessors will ensure as best they can that the circumstances are right for the test to take place, that the appropriate briefing is carried out, and the test environment is suitable.

Whichever, psychometric tests are indicators and no more. They are an aid to assist the understanding of the operational qualities and actions an individual is most likely to invoke in various circumstances.

There is an analogy with horoscopes. The descriptive words can apply to many people types. It is not an exact science.

The big danger is that a manager may have already come to a

conclusion about one of his reports and looks to the psychometric test for supportive evidence. It is possible to interpret tests in differing ways and is therefore not too difficult to fit the results to expectations.

External pressures

Now to the last of the more visible and likely difficulties you may encounter in the quest to gain success and satisfaction all round from the implementation of a performance management process.

What if your business is subjected to external pressures beyond its control and it has to adjust? What if the industry is subjected to unexpected forces that require it to re-shape, to review its operating costs, its employee earnings ratios and so on.

You will have to make decisions from a thorough review of all elements of the particular circumstance created by the external pressure.

This situation is probably the most difficult to deal with because there is no clear-cut action to take and no right or wrong decision. The right one is to make a decision on some action whatever it is. The wrong one is to be complacent and take no action, to see no problem. You may determine not to invoke the action until a certain trigger point, but you must be prepared, ready for the time to strike.

Like a chameleon, the hidden threat from an innocent-looking external change can be difficult to spot and easy to miss. If your business is dependent on oil and oil becomes scarce or trebles in price overnight and is the first item on the evening news, you will be pretty much aware.

But if a new competitor starts up in a small way, you may not be too concerned initially, especially if you are the biggest in the industry and are doing business with all the customers in the industry as you have for the last 50 years.

You won't know necessarily what that competitor is doing. You may not have even given it too much thought. Yet this competitor may have a long-term strategy to take your number one slot from you.

You must clearly have your ear to the ground, be tuned in to everything going on in your industry and its environment. But that should of course be a given.

The key, the absolute key when learning of some issue of potential threat, is to:

- ensure that you share the issue with everyone (it is not a management cop out, but a genuine awareness communication)
- ensure they all understand the significance
- get the buy-in to deal with it
- involve everyone in solution seeking (an acceptable buzzword!) – have you become complacent?
- maintain focus on achieving the objective.

External pressures will of course occur unexpectedly, which is why it is so important not to become complacent with success, to have contingency plans in place, and to play 'What if' scenario games.

As an example, just when your new people management approach has won the buy-in from all the people in the business, and they have pulled out all the stops, and your business is the slickest in the industry, producing more sploggits per fraction of a man-hour than the nearest competitor, The Chancellor has lunch with the Bank of England, the pound moves the wrong way big time and your export orders are under threat.

Your big competitor in Belgium is able to soak up more orders and is better placed to sell in Europe because of the strength of the pound and physical location. Up until now you have been competitive on price but with that shift in exchange rates, well, Belgium are poised for an attack.

Or perhaps your number one revenue-earning customer tells you that as a result of market information, they are having to launch a new product that you are unable to supply and will begin running down stocks of your product as of next week.

You now have to explain to your highly committed converts that all their efforts will not yield the rewards they might expect – in fact they are lucky to have jobs at all. Some may not for much longer.

154

Employee rewards and benefits are usually the first to be impacted.

So what of your freshly implemented, common-sense process now?

Well, the fact is of course that it would have been a darn site worse without the new process, and these things do happen and will always happen. Mr Sod and Mr Murphy are great buddies, they like nothing better than working in tandem. One of them can have a big impact, but the results of their dual effort becomes exponential.

With performance management and business procedures active and effective in your organisation, you will be far better placed to deal with such external pressures than trying to react after the stable door is unbolted.

However, there is another tool in the box that will enhance your process and help to maintain your competitive position.

Contingency plans

The top man in the organisation has a responsibility alongside that of determining the mission statement, of painting the black picture before it might arrive.

Contingency plans (which are now being called 'business continuity plans'!) are an essential part of the tool box. The 'What if' scenario games must be played. New 'What if' scenarios must always be developed and played out.

This is a part of real culture change – being prepared to face adversity, rather than kicking against it like a spoilt child, when it arrives.

However, as with the acceptance of the need for performance management, it will be an uphill struggle to get a tick in the box for the need for a contingency planning programme.

The reason for reticence is of course obvious.

To invest in planning for something that may or may not happen is not readily easy to justify.

It all depends on the size of the risk and the effect of the consequence.

One company I worked for took contingency planning seriously. It was a way of life. I found it difficult to take seriously when I first joined and encountered a review of an internal agreement between two departments. My department had to show documented procedures for the archiving of electronic technical documentation in the event of fire, flood and whatever.

The Facilities Manager had similarly to provide documented procedures to ensure business continuance in the event of a total fire.

Yet the building was all but brand new and constructed of fire resistant, flame-retardant, fire-proof materials and all computer rooms were protected by halon gas (permitted in those days). The building constructors said the building could not burn. Any fire would be local and quickly contained.

One night, a fire started, and within an hour the entire building was razed to the ground. The words of the building constructors still echo in my ears: 'That just shouldn't have happened'.

The Facilities Manager executed his contingency plan and within three days the business was fully operating again from its planned alternative temporary site, and our electronic technical documentation was in full use having been retrieved from its remote archive.

My scepticism disappeared. I became a convert, a supporter, a promoter of contingency planning, or its more recently adopted buzzword, business continuity planning.

Contingency planning – part of your life

Contingency planning should be a live activity throughout the organisation. All departments should be required to determine which parts of their area of the business require contingency plans. Plans should be developed and tested in accordance with an appropriate schedule. contingency plans must not be put in the safe for the rainy-day disaster. People must be trained in their application in readiness for the potential event.

The most effective time to review contingency plans and the need for new ones, is when the business is thriving. This is the time to prepare for the next downturn.

It is a natural human attitude to become complacent in times of a thriving economy or a booming business. Yet that is precisely the time to look for the black picture and determine a survival and conquest route.

Within the business process there should be a procedure to determine contingency plans along the following lines:

- Review areas of the business that have the potential to seriously impact the business if something went wrong. (Murphy's Law no. 3 – 'If it can go wrong it will.')
- Develop and document a contingency plan for each identified activity.
- Train all related people in execution of each plan.
- Develop a schedule appropriate for each of the above ('It will happen when you least expect it' – a law from one of Murphy's relations) to ensure they are up-to-date.

Once again, if you develop a ready-to-run contingency plan for each potential disaster, you are in the best position to recover should the disaster become a reality. You have done your best.

To reward or not to reward?

Should performance be linked to reward? That is the question.

The merits for and against are many and whichever view you take you will consider that yours is the right one. Common sense tells you of course that if you passionately believe in something then deciding to go with it is the right decision. It has to be.

The consequences are myriad and dire. You cannot afford to get it wrong.

To determine which route you take you must know why you are doing it. In order to answer that one, consideration should be given to the following. Do you:

- fully understand the consequences (long as well as short term)
- have a well-developed strategy
- fully understand the cost implications

- have a contingency plan
- have a review team set up and scheduled
- fully understand the alternative option and are absolutely sure which one is right for your business
- have support from the top and from the majority of people in the business.

Everything else is mechanical, a process to be unfolded.

You need to be ready to make quick decisions too – you cannot have foreseen all the issues that will surface, but you will need to address them quickly or confidence in you and your process will drain fast.

If you do go for linking reward to performance you may need to have a plan for breaking the link if it fails. Make it top of the agenda for the annual review.

My personal view is that performance management is the tool to use to get things done in line with business strategy. Reward belongs to a different strategy, aligned to success and affordability. There should be no link. But that is a personal view.

If reward is judged to be a required link to performance levels, then surely it is better to do this as a one-off bonus per year rather than linking it to salary?

Very much a personal view, but I believe that the best value from performance management systems stops at the review in terms of evidence and evidential words. Maybe a financial bonus is appropriate – I do not see any added value in ratings or in linking to salaries – only heartache and added difficulties that run and run.

However, both strategies should be fully owned, warts and all, success and failure, by those at the top of the business.

Summary of Opportunities

- You must get business buy-in to support the need to implement a performance management process and Quality System.

- Cloning of people has not yet been achieved. People are all different. They have different emotions and ways of operating. Those who understand their people will reap the best rewards from those people, in the long term.

- Listen to the latest buzzwords and their intended meaning, but you don't have to go with them.

- Invest big time in recruitment whenever the opportunity arises – it will pay you back handsomely.

- Expect the unexpected – have an effective contingency plan for all eventualities.

- Do everything possible to get the best people under you – you are a reflection of them.

- Determine the business stance on linking reward to performance. Understand the significance. Know the consequences.

Index